Praise for *Bring Out the Best in Every Employee*

We all know that the leader of the future will be a person who knows how to ask. *Bring Out the Best* will get you started—it does the asking for you!

—Marshall Goldsmith
Harvard Business Review's #1 Leadership Thinker

A motivated human being gets consistently reliable output from themselves and others. Give me a workforce in which even 60 percent fit the above—and I will move mountains! *Bring Out the Best* shows you how to do just that.

—Davis L. Holloway, United States Air Force, Retired

Empathy is not abstract—it's concrete! It is teachable, and matters bottom line. Let *Bring Out the Best* help you connect less to technology and more to those you lead.

—Dr. Sarah Konrath, Assistant Research Professor
University of Michigan

At Maquet we fix hearts for a living. *Bring Out the Best* shows you how to engage the heart of your team!

—Raoul Quintero, President, Maquet Medical Systems

We're no longer victims of our past—and you can be the leader you want to be! This book will show you how to be present, to bring out the best in everyone you care for.

—Dr. Terri Egan, Associate Professor, Pepperdine University

To be an effective leader you need to have a heart big enough to take in all the people you are trying to lead, yet wise enough not to crowd out your loved ones. Let *Bring Out the Best* show you how.

—Dr. Dan Saferstein, Sports Psychologist

The foundational research for *Bring Out the Best* is right on—our people want communication, feedback, and not just autonomy, but the authority to try! Read this book; engagement happens one moment at a time.

—Troy Van Hauen, VP Human Resources, The Maschhoffs

Take care of your energy as if it were the most important resource on the planet, because it is—it's all you have! You are reading this book because you care about yourself. Continue caring!

> —Natalie Brown, MS, C.S.C.S., Fitness Quest 10

As leaders we like to think we control everything, and it's just not true—externals now drive the business. Learn to let go, learn to bring out the best in every employee!

> —Jim Farley, Group VP Global Marketing,
> Sales & Service, Ford Motor Company

One of the things we'll look back on 30 years from now is that this no-normal world has forced a higher quality of leadership than any other era in history. *Bring Out the Best* is the ultimate leader's handbook to that higher ground!

> —Howard Morgan, Managing Director,
> The Leadership Research Institute

One Fortune organization once reported that it interviewed 1,000,000 annually, that it hired 125,000 of them—and yet, that their net productivity gain was only 15,000 employees! This paradox demonstrates the imperative to learning how to bring out the best in every employee you have.

> —C.D. "Hoop" Morgan III
> Founder and Chairman, The Forté Institute

What's different today? The entire world, and everyone in it, is in the midst of a change curve. No one is exempt, and the productivity we need from our workforce is going to have to increase. This book is the leader's guide to starting that process, and to stopping the self-imposed barriers of the ego.

> —Chuck Sykes, President and CEO, Sykes Enterprises

Today, it's complexity that makes it tough on a leader—and an engaged team a nonnegotiable. *Bring Out the Best* shows you how to expand your capacity without adding a single headcount!

> —Tim Srock, VP Human Resources
> McLaren Regional Medical Center

BRING OUT THE
BEST
IN
EVERY
EMPLOYEE

HOW TO ENGAGE YOUR WHOLE TEAM BY MAKING EVERY LEADERSHIP MOMENT COUNT

DON BROWN
BILL HAWKINS

New York   Chicago   San Francisco   Lisbon   London   Madrid   Mexico City
Milan   New Delhi   San Juan   Seoul   Singapore   Sydney   Toronto

The **McGraw·Hill** Companies

1 2 3 4 5 6 7 8 9 0   DOC/DOC   1 8 7 6 5 4 3 2

ISBN 978-0-07-178713-0
MHID 0-07-178713-5

e-ISBN 978-0-07-178714-7
e-MHID 0-07-178714-3

McGraw-Hill books are available at special quantity discounts to use as premiums and sales promotions or for use in corporate training programs. To contact a representative, please e-mail us at bulksales@mcgraw-hill.com.

This book is printed on acid-free paper.

Library of Congress Cataloging-in-Publication Data
Brown, Don
    Bring out the best in every employee : how to engage your whole team by making every leadership moment count / Don Brown. — 1
        p. cm.
    ISBN 978-0-07-178713-0 (alk. paper)
    ISBN 0-07-178713-5 (alk. paper)
    1. Supervision of employees. 2. Leadership. 3. Employee motivation. 4. Teams in the workplace. I. Hawkins, Bill.- II. Title.
    HF5549.12.B776 2012
    658.3'14—dc23
                                                                    2012033480

We have had the honor of working with some pretty big players in the field of leadership. Indeed, much of this book was inspired by them and by their work, and we take great pride now in helping others work on bringing out the best in their people. While the rest of us "work on it," there is one person who embodies the habits you'll soon discover.

All who know him agree that a moment with Davis L. Holloway moves you to be a better manager yourself. We dedicate this work to him. When it comes to bringing out the best, Davis is The Natural.

CONTENTS

Contents

FOREWORD

Don Brown, Bill Hawkins, and I share a *lot* of history. It is therefore an honor and a pleasure for me to write this foreword to their new book, *Bring Out the Best in Every Employee*. Bill and I go back more years than I care to remember; we even roomed together in college, and then moved on to decades of successful collaboration in the Marshall Goldsmith Group. Don and I also claim a significant life event in common, and share two very powerful professional anchors: the relentless affinity for data, and an undying affection for the same mentor in Dr. Paul Hersey.

To anyone who will listen I proudly tell the story of how Dr. Hersey gave me my start in the business of leadership. Don got his start from "Doc" Hersey as well. In the late 1970s I was finishing my Ph.D. at UCLA and applied for a teaching position at USIU in San Diego. During my interviews I met Dr. Hersey, the Dean of the School of Business. He asked me why I wanted to be a college professor. I enthusiastically answered, "I love teaching." Paul then asked if I wouldn't prefer the opportunity to teach without the bother of homework, grading, or faculty meetings. He also mentioned that at times he was so busy he had to turn down work and asked if I thought I could do what he did—for a single day's pay that matched my previous month's take-home! Paul gave me my start, and the rest is history.

In the mid 1980s Dr. Hersey brought Don Brown into the Center for Leadership Studies to run its day-to-day operations. Don stayed in-house with Paul for three years—and has remained Doc's top affiliate every year since. Dr. Hersey knows talent.

Period. Countless others of the highest caliber got their start with the Center. Does the name *Ken Blanchard* sound familiar?

During Don's time with Dr. Hersey he conducted research toward a masters in management, and although I was long gone from the Center, Don asked me to join Paul on his research review board. His insights into sales training and coaching were so stunning that I asked him if he would like to do a book together. The result was last year's *What Got You Here Won't Get You There—in Sales!*

In *Bring Out the Best in Every Employee* that dedication to data as the way to simple truth is no less evident. We all know that the leader of the future will be a person who knows how to ask; the leader of the future won't know enough to tell people what to do. The no-normal world that unfolds on the following pages is changing much too quickly for any one person to be smart enough to keep up with. The effective leader of the future will regularly ask for feedback and ideas—yet many of us still fail to ask what our people want and need from us. Whether fearing the answers or lacking the time and focus to personally inquire, we don't ask.

Bring Out the Best in Every Employee will get you started— it does the asking for you! At every organizational level, in every corner of the globe, you can learn what your people want you to know, want you to do, and how to go about it. My colleagues have asked about that "one thing" you can do to matter in the lives of your people, what to stop, what to start, and what to continue doing in order to engage the core of your team.

You will be compelled by the writing to take in *Bring Out the Best in Every Employee* in a single sitting. It's that good. My advice? Take your time. Soak in the dynamics of what you face as a leader in the new millennium. Discover where you should be focusing your leadership efforts for maximum return. Get yourself ready to lead in the moment, and master a powerful leader's protocol to engage the core of your team. Learn to bring out the best in all those that count on you, in all those that matter to you.

Marshall Goldsmith

Marshall Goldsmith is the bestselling author of MOJO *and* What Got You Here Won't Get You There—in Sales! *and one of the top 10 most influential thinkers in the world.*

ACKNOWLEDGMENTS

Labor of love: work for the sake of one's own enjoyment.

Writing a book truly is a labor of love. Ask any author; the process can be life changing! Ask any author, too; a transformative event such as this is made possible by the support and contributions of others. We would like to take this opportunity to express our appreciation to those that made this labor of love a reality. Thank you for *your* labor. Thank you for giving of your time and experience, and for pushing back when we might have been "wrong but certain." Thank you for caring and sharing, for helping bring out the best in this labor of love: *Natalie Brown, Ron Campbell, Donya Dickerson, Terri Egan, Jim Farley, Marshall Goldsmith, Paul Hersey, Davis Holloway, Sara Konrath, Sarah McArthur, Hoop Morgan, Howard Morgan, Raoul Quintero, Dan Saferstein, Tim Srock, Lauren Swartz, Chuck Sykes, Troy Van Hauen.*

To those closest to us:

Don Brown: To Colleen, Natalie, Kelly, and Katie—To paraphrase one of my favorites, "You make me want to be a better man-ager." Thank you for being there, for being patient, and for being you. *Amor y besos.*

Bill Hawkins: Special thanks to my wife, Linda, the glue who holds the family together while I'm 30,000 feet in the air in another time zone. To my daughters, Sarah and Sandy, and my son, Dave, I'm so proud of each of you. I love you very much.

INTRODUCTION
". . . AND THE BOOKS YOU READ"

As with most men and women in leadership and managerial roles today, there is most likely an abundance of structure in place for the management side of your job: policies, procedures, performance management, processes, approvals, scheduling, forecasting. It's a job just to keep up, keep pace and comply with it all. And just how engaging (for you *or* your team members) is that side of what you do every day?

Now let's look at the leadership side of your job. Leadership is essentially the process of influence, of getting someone else to do something and feel good about it. What kind of structure or design does your employer put in place for the *human* interactions you engage in on its behalf? Our experience (and our research) tells us that the answer to the question of how much guidance you get is not much. In many organizations, it approaches zero. For us, the human side of *your* job targets just one goal: bringing out the best in every employee.

What we offer today is a clear, global, research-based voice for any team and what it wants of a leader. We've recruited expert perspective, and *you* profit from their views: Jim Farley, Ford Motor Company; Raoul Quintero, Maquet Medical Systems; Chuck Sykes, Sykes Enterprises; Sara Konrath, University of Michigan Institute for Social Research; Marshall Goldsmith, the world's number-one leadership thinker; Howard Morgan, global top-50 coach; Tim Srock, McLaren Medical; Troy Van Hauen, the Maschhoffs; Davis Holloway, U.S. Air Force, retired, and

Southwest Airlines; Hoop Morgan, the Forte Institute; Terri Egan, Pepperdine University; Dan Saferstein, sports psychologist; and Natalie Brown, Fitness Quest 10. We have synthesized research and expertise into a powerful leader's protocol of learning to be present to meet your team's needs for communication, feedback, and autonomy.

We can most efficiently equip you for the power of what's to come by answering questions that might be entering your mind at this moment:

1. The source. How do we know what your people want from you?
2. The setting. Why do you need a protocol for leadership? Why now?
3. The X factor. Is there one element that trumps all others?
4. The return. What's in it for you and your people?
5. The way. What is it that you need to be able to do in order to get the return?
6. The fuel. How do you succeed with all that you have on your plate?

The Source: How Do We Know What Your People Want from You?

We know what your people want from you because we asked them. Research gave us over 6,000 confidential responses to four very simple questions:

1. If you could tell your boss just one thing about his or her leadership of you, what would you say?
2. In leading you, what do you want your boss to *start* doing?

3. In leading you, what do you want your boss to *stop* doing?
4. In leading you, what do you want your boss to *continue* doing?

The responses we received came from every corner of the globe—from Asia-Pacific and the Americas to Europe, the Middle East, and Africa—and from every organizational perspective, from C-level to line level.

And then we took it a step further to make sure we would provide you with the most accurate and meaningful interpretation possible. We conducted separate in-depth interviews with thought leaders, executives, managers, academics, and practitioners to add their opinion to our own. They taught us a great deal about what's different for all of us leading today, and what it might be like to be a leader in another 10 years.

The Setting: Why Do You Need a Protocol for Leadership? Why Now?

Perhaps we can best illustrate our collective working environment by pulling a single descriptive word from the title of Reuters' consumer attitude reports over the last 16 months: stagnation, downturn, slowdown, falling, stagnant, concern, temporary, slowing, rising, worry, dismal, weaken, slow, very slow, tumbles, unchanged.

By all accounts, leading today is very different from the way it was six to eight years ago (you know that). The world of eight years *from now* is going to be almost unrecognizable when compared to *right now*. A culture of never-ending change has settled upon us. The concept of management control has irretrievably departed, and the setting will be one of things happening to us and not as planned by us. The entire world is on a change curve right now, and that curve promises to get steeper. That's why we need a leader's protocol right now.

The X Factor: Is There One Element That Trumps All Others?

The X factor of unlimited power in effective influence is empathy. *Empathy* means that others believe that you understand and that you care. Period. Our research demonstrates that nothing else is more central to their discretionary effort. Notice that we didn't say that you agree with them. Simply understanding, both intellectually and emotionally, and caring about their circumstances is directly connected to how engaged they become in performing for you.

The Return: What's in It for You or for Your People?

"What's in it for you or your people?" is the easiest question to answer. For you, the return on bringing out the best in others is directly correlated with the output of your team in the near term and long term. At its most basic, it is about creating capacity without additional headcount. If you can be more effective in your influence efforts, your people engage more fully. When they engage more fully, they give more of themselves and utilize more of their potential. When they utilize more of their potential or capability, performance increases, sometimes exponentially.

We all know of individuals who have checked out or "retired on the job." There's a line of performance at about 30 to 40 percent of their potential. (See Figure I.1.) They know right where it is, and they also know that if they don't drop below that level of minimal output, they will remain employed. Experience also shows that there is another line at about 80 percent of personal potential that represents the performance we can sustain over time when we are fully motivated and engaged. This delta, the difference between getting 30 percent of someone and getting 80 percent of someone, is your return on leadership and bringing out the best for both of you. You benefit from maximum output, and your team gets

FIGURE I.1   The Return on Leadership

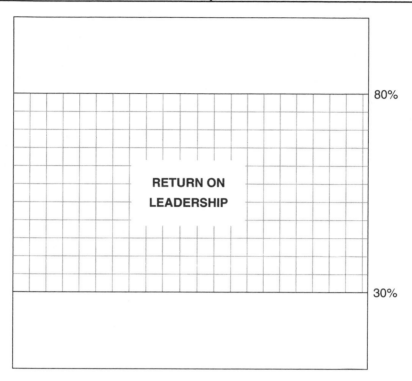

maximum involvement, enjoyment, and engagement. Let's be honest. How happy can someone be as a charter member of the 30 percent club? Not very.

The Way: What Is It You Need to Be Able to Do in Order to Get the Return?

It might sound simple, but in order to get the return, you need to be able to be present. Have you ever noticed that for some reason we feel free to do just about anything while we're driving a car? We talk on the phone, eat, smoke, text, shave, curl eyelashes, or even floss our teeth, all while controlling a significant mass traveling at terrific speed in traffic. Have you also looked around you lately while you're out in a restaurant and noticed a couple at another table, both focused on their iPhone and not a word passing between them?

Why do we do it? Because this is the era of multitasking! Electronic productivity tools abound to help us keep up, and 90 percent of us don't even use the on/off buttons anymore (you don't either, do you?). It's one thing to work on increasing personal efficiency, but what about the bleed-over into interpersonal efficiency? Can we apply the same tactics in reference to multitasking when we aren't alone? The answer is that we do it all the time, and it's an empathy killer. There is no room for interpersonal multitasking. Go for *effective*, not efficient.

The Fuel: How Do You Succeed with All That You Have on Your Plate?

The fuel for effective leadership in a world gone mad is generating and focusing your passion for what you do as a leader. There is a lot you can't control today in your organizational environment—probably most of it. But you can control you—your thoughts, your feelings, your conduct, and they are all connected. By far, the most important thing we teach in this book is how to be happy and passionate about what you do as a leader. We don't mean switch jobs to do something that you love (you're going to do those things anyway). A few hundred pages from now you will have in your hand the key to being passionate about leading others, in the job you have, right now. It will fuel you, and it will fuel those around you.

> *The only difference between who you are today*
> *and who you will be 5 years from now are*
> *the people you meet*, and the books you read.
> —Charlie "Tremendous" Jones

A few hundred pages from now you will be a different you, a different leader. In depth and detail we cover how to get more capacity from your team, without more headcount. You will learn about the "empathy crash of 2000," and how to avoid it in your life. You will discover the best of 6,000 insights from around the world, what your people would tell you if you would only ask, and specifically what they want you to do. You will have new insights into understanding yourself and your interactions, where to target your intentions, and how to be comfortable being present with others. In these pages you will learn how to bring out the best!

A NEW ERA

We are in a business world in flux, in a change curve that's global, not local, with fallout for you as an individual and powerful implications for you as a leader of others. For example:

- **There is no new normal.** Find out why we have no choice but to elevate capacity without adding headcount, to get more done with the same people.
- **Time and technology.** Discover the impact of the twenty-first century on how we interact with one another, or don't, and what it means to each of us personally.
- **Implications in leading.** Prepare yourself for what's here, and what's coming because you're the one responsible for the output of others.

CHAPTER 1

No-Normal: Capacity Without Headcount

L et's begin your journey to bringing out the best in others. Let's start by considering the macro, which is the set of *global* dynamics that seem to be affecting every one of us no matter where we are on the planet—the new normal. You hear about it everywhere. The *new normal* continues to resonate on radio, television, and social media. You've seen it on ABC News, Fox, National Public Radio, and even the *McKinsey Quarterly*. The tales of woe follow a similar theme: lower starting wages, vanishing job security, pay cuts of 5, 10, or even 20 percent, furloughs, unpaid work, unaccustomed thrift, double-digit unemployment, underemployment, five-figure job cuts, and punitive new procedures for the lending and borrowing of capital. Conventional wisdom would have you believe that our collective economy and existence has finally settled into a new set of norms and expectations.

We'd like to propose a change in perspective to that of no normal!

Normal [*nawr-muhl*] :
Conforming to or establishing a common standard or type . . . the acknowledged average, commonplace, customary, habitual, natural, orderly, ordinary, prevalent, regular, routine, run-of-the-mill or typical.

3

Are you witnessing anything today that conforms to the above definition or synonyms for the term *normal*? Is there anything habitual, orderly, or routine about what you see going on around you? We would submit that normal has yet to gel again. Just when we think things have settled down, a new frontier for chaos opens up. Change that was once seen as a well-deserved realignment of an antiquated rust belt or dot-com paradigms now bleeds over into public and private education, state and municipal government, housing and construction, and even whole societies and cultures around the world.

So there is no normal. The consensus seems to be that it could take another decade before any new normal settles out of the clutter and discord that make up our daily lives. And this isn't just our opinion. We mention in our introduction that we conducted in-depth interviews with thought leaders, executives, academics, and practitioners alike, and their views are presented here. From the formal interviews we conducted for this book, as well as dozens of off-the-record conversations we've had with executives and managers in our client organizations, the resounding chorus is one of often not having a clue as to what is coming next. Where once the job at the highest level was to plan and execute, today it is simply to create readiness to adapt, to respond, and to essentially prepare for possibilities. This scary environment of externals driving the enterprise is hardly a normal scenario by any definition. No-normal rules.

Understanding is the first step toward acceptance and adaptation. What do we know at a macro level about how to define this new era? Three standout variables characterize business dynamics today: growth, change, and relationships. These words aren't new to you; these ideas in one form or another have been part of our organizational lexicon for a long time. The form is the key, what *is* new is the very *nature* of the growth, change, and relationships that you see. Let's take a look.

Growth

Believe it or not, there is still a great deal of growth taking place these days, just not here, just not in the United States, or perhaps not in the shape or form we are accustomed to. For a long time, strategic planning meant looking at last year's financial results, adding some factor of 10 or 20 percent, and calling it *targeted growth*. Expansion, emergence, consolidation, and connection define growth today. Growth no longer takes the form of simply striving for more of everything. Growth can mean a shift in complexity. Growth can be seen as dynamic movement from one stage or form to another.

Let's look at a first example of what growth means today, in the BRIC (Brazil, Russia, India, and China) markets. These markets are emerging areas of tremendous economic, political, and social transformation, and they will continue to be for the foreseeable future. One high-tech CEO (whose name you would instantly recognize) was asked not that long ago what his organization was up to in India. His response was short and to the point: "We're not up to anything; they don't buy what we make."

That's no longer the case. The economies of Brazil, Russia, India, and China now rank seventh, eleventh, ninth, and second, respectively, in GDP, according to the CIA *World Factbook*. And these four economic engines rank fifth, eighth, second, and first in terms of their population, which is their consumer base. Either way, these economies are now forces to be reckoned with. Their growth cannot be ignored. One of the "big three" U.S. automobile manufacturers is currently targeting a significant reduction in the number of retail dealers that represent it here in the United States (let's face it, they all are). That same brand is also currently striving to add some 1,300 dealers in these developing markets around the world; *this is what growth looks like today!*

In a no-normal state, growth often means consolidation. Organizations still become larger, just not the way they used to. Building new plants, hiring massive numbers, investing heavily in research and development are now seen as excessive and unacceptable risk. It's better to acquire another organization to grow by 40 percent in staffing and revenue. It's better to acquire the small entrepreneurial company that has developed the latest game-changing technology rather than develop it in house. Growth strategies today, like any investing, are all about capturing as much up side as possible. But even more importantly, it's about minimizing the down capture. First, do no harm.

A final manifestation of growth to consider is perhaps counterintuitive and has to do with simultaneous increases in efficiency and complexity. The work we all have to do is growing. More with less is a very real mantra for just about anyone, and perhaps even more *for* less if you've taken a pay cut. We've all had to become much more efficient, just as our jobs are expanding! There's nothing mysterious here. It's a simple fact of employment and capacity. We have been losing jobs in the workforce in the United States and Europe, and even across Asia. The total numbers vary based on the particular day and the data source, but let's turn data into usable information. Tens of millions of people are out of work. If you're not working, you're not spending. If you are afraid of losing your job (or your market share), you are afraid of spending. Consumers (and companies) hunker down and hold back when they're uncertain of their income. Unlike public sector strategies of spending as a way out, in private we get thrifty when money gets tight.

And what effect will this reduced demand have on capacity then? Any "right-sizing" of the workforce is a balancing act of capacity with current demand, and we're not done yet, not by a long shot. Companies and countries are still paring back.

Industrial capacity utilization is still at one of its lowest levels ever, and, given excess capacity, we won't be rehiring. And while we right-size the labor force, we also bring additional pressure to bear on getting better, faster, and cheaper. This applies to all of us, companies, contractors, governments; here and abroad. All of us.

But wait, becoming more efficient is a *good* thing, right? Not for jobs. Employers will add hours before headcount every time. For decades it was believed that labor had the upper hand, and as workweeks contracted, the workforce grew. Now the trend has reversed: People are working more hours, not fewer. And if we get only 1 percent more efficient, that's 1.5 million jobs that won't come back—ever. No matter how you look at it, the math is working against us. If we lose 20 percent of any labor pool and then gain back 20 percent, we're still down. Think about it. If we lose 20 percent, we then need a 25 percent gain to get back level. If we lose 50 percent, we need *100* percent employment growth just to get back to where we started!

So our labor force is becoming smaller but more efficient. What does that do to complexity? It causes *no-normal* growth in the complexity of what we do every day. Let's face it. People go away, but the work doesn't, and therefore the complexity of our jobs as leaders expands. We all have to know more about financials, demographics, operations, psychology, law, and government, and the pace of learning is accelerating!

Growth is a significant part of a no-normal economy. It's just a new kind of growth. It comes in new forms. It happens somewhere else. It happens through consolidation and acquisition rather than organic expansion. It is happening with very low tolerance for risk or down capture. It causes our jobs to expand, not our workforce. It demands a significant increase in personal capacity with a zero increase in headcount.

Change

Change essentially means *to make different*. Change has been a huge part of our professional lives up until now, and traditional change dynamics are still here, although the cycles have become shorter and shorter. What has changed about change is, again, the *nature* of the beast. Through our interviews with executives of global organizations, we've learned two very important lessons about change in a no-normal world; first, it's an interactive global curve; there's nothing isolated about it. The second lesson is that change is now all about an externalization of events—things happening to us.

With respect to the global change curve, every context and continent has undergone change in the last decade, and managing this change hasn't been easy by any means. What is the difference today? We're never in it alone. Think about any given "day in the life": bankruptcy proceedings for what was once the largest company on the planet, a cruise ship capsizing and killing dozens in the twenty-first century, oil rigs spilling millions of gallons of crude oil, the entire national economy of Greece melting down and fellow Eurozone countries bailing the country out, new nations being born, new big kids on the block, the beginnings of democracy where dictatorship long ruled, tsunamis wreaking havoc across an entire people, modern day piracy on the high seas, the very real possibility of nuclear weapons in the hands of many, not just a few. The nature of change has morphed into one of everyday occurrence, of pervasive examples that all interact with one another.

Consider the dynamics of perhaps a single, powerful global change curve—pervasive change bringing pervasive opportunity, but also pervasive uncertainty. Uncertainty brings reticence. Reticence brings delay in adding new people, in starting new ventures, in taking risk. You know you need more capacity. And you know you won't get more headcount.

8

What do we mean then by change and the externalization of events? The global curve tells us that it's happening everywhere. *Externalization* means that it's happening to us outside in. The pace of change is so rapid that a cumulative effect of change has kicked in. A critical mass of change has found its own momentum, so that change isn't planned anymore. Change usually isn't even expected or anticipated anymore. Change can hardly be imagined anymore, let alone foreseen. Change today can only be accommodated and responded to. If you can't imagine it, you can't foresee it. If you can't foresee it, you can't plan for it. If you can't plan for it, how do you prepare for it? Through agility and resilience. Through the capacity to respond quickly and without sustaining mortal injury to the enterprise.

The new capacity we need is not in the form of more people. The capacity growth we need lies within the people we already have. It is all we're going to get right now.

Relationships

The final no-normal variable for consideration is the nature of our relationships going forward. Think about it for a moment. Take a deep breath.

What does pervasive and unforeseen change tend to do to relationships? What impact will it have on certainty? On trust? On permanence? On forgiveness? It will crush them:

○ Organizational loyalty to employees is more conditional than ever.

○ Employee loyalty to one's employer is more tenuous than ever.

○ The number of economic hostages is higher than ever.

○ The number of organizations using the liquidation of human assets as a means to short-term earnings has never been higher.

○ Commitment, on either side, is at an all-time low.

9

Does that sound like a marriage made in heaven? What odds do you give to "divorce" as the ultimate outcome? Even if we do stay together because we have no other option, what are the odds that we are getting all we can out of the relationship? As an employee, how much vulnerability will I be willing to risk in uncertain times? As an employer, how much of the potential of our human resource do you think is being captured right now? Unfortunately, the answer is probably quite low, but the flipside is that we have a fantastic opportunity to increase our team's capacity without adding headcount.

Our people are *waiting* to be engaged. Our research for this book makes this very clear. We spoke with followers around the globe to ask them, and they are *waiting* to give more discretionary performance. We *can* get significant increases in capacity without adding numbers. Capacity without headcount is doable. *You* can do it by simply bringing out the best in those people you count on for results.

New Era—New Perspectives

A great deal of research and discussion and many interviews have been organized into a treasure trove of new perspectives to match this new business era. Throughout this book, you will learn from the voices of several individuals uniquely qualified and uniquely experienced to help us understand this new era.

What follows are verbatim observations from:

- **James D. Farley, group vice president, global marketing, sales and service, Ford Motor Company:** Jim Farley is Ford's first single global leader of marketing, sales and service.
- **Raoul Quintero, president and CEO, Maquet Medical Systems:** Raoul has over 30 years of experience driving sales growth in the medical device industry.

○ **Charles E. Sykes, president, Sykes Enterprises:** Chuck Sykes leads the organization that carries his name, close to 50,000 people in North America, Latin America, Europe, and Asia delivering contact center, product assistance, and telehealth services.

We initiated the discussion with two questions for the three men. What they had to say was very powerful:

Bring Out the Best: At a macro view of the economy, what's different about today versus 10 years ago, and what will be different in another 10 years?

Jim Farley: The main difference today is that the externals now drive the business. We as leaders like to think that we control everything, but that's just not true anymore. The big change is what is happening to us and around us—the externals. Your second question, how is this going to be different in another 10 years, is that the externals will be more and more important. We will have less discretionary control over our company's future, because more and more will be done to us. No one would've predicted a commodity crisis or the emergence of the middle class in Brazil, India, and Indonesia. No one would have predicted the collapse of the financial system, nor does it matter.

For us in the automobile business, one of the externals that is emerging involves population growth and city center density rising to a point where emissions control and fuel economy and consumption will be the primary driver of buying automobiles around the globe. We will see mass electrification in our industry in the next few years—the electrification of the automobile. It will affect every part of our business.

Raoul Quintero: What is really different about today in medical equipment? For me it's the fall of the transformational leader. At one time there appeared to be individuals who were building the visions and goals. They were offering support and stimulation to an organization to create a future. Ten years later we find a transactional leader where every decision seems to pretty much revolve around a profit and loss responsibility, where everything is measured in currency. There was once a lot more room for error—but our collective margin for error has been reduced dramatically today.

Ten years ago we were a smaller entrepreneurial organization among a collection of small entrepreneurial efforts within the company. Each of us a small component of a big company, we could have been a rounding error with no real significance, just a little piece of the much bigger picture. If we missed our targets, no one got badly hurt. If we overshot our targets, no one much celebrated either. In the bigger picture, we were no more meaningful than rounding up or down. Fast-forward 10 years of consolidation and integration, and now we are a half a billion dollars. We're nobody's rounding error anymore. If we don't hit what we say, everyone knows it; everyone *feels* it. If I make a mistake now, the entire company has a big problem. I think that same clustering will continue to take place, and that's why organizational forgiveness seems such a thing of the past. Everything is scrutinized. Everything is important to everyone today.

Chuck Sykes: It's interesting, Don, because in considering your questions, what is and will be different for both external and internal to the company, almost the same words come to mind. When you think about it, a number of years ago we were going through our own period of globalization at Sykes, and it was exhilarating. That is still occurring right now, but the difference right now is that the entire world, and everyone in it, is in the midst of his or her own change curve.

You know how challenging that can be just inside of a single organization when you're trying to lead change, and you're trying to focus on how you communicate the message, how you get everyone on board, how you get people to follow. But that pervasive of a change creates very high degrees of anxiety. Just looking at the world right now, everybody keeps trying to blame everybody else for everything that's going on. And the way I see it, is, look, the world is just in the midst of a change curve. You can look for blame all you want, but it isn't really going to be there. No fault, just anxiety.

For the most part, the collective uncertainty that exists today is something I've never personally experienced in my professional time of leading. Even when we were going through change and globalization, what was interesting was that you could still look at the change and say, "Oh, the world is getting more global." Even though that creates some tension, at least it's a change that's anticipated and known to a degree. Today you pick an area, and it's changing. Technology is changing, government is changing, countries are changing, tax structures are probably going to change, attitudes and just society in general are all changing. Almost every aspect is in a state of flux. I've just never experienced anything like it, and I don't think anyone has who's alive today.

And I agree with you, by the way; right now in the midst of this change curve, there is no normal. I think we are going to emerge out of the curve, but not for at least another five years.

Jim Farley: Probably the next biggest shift in play for us in automotive will be the growth of our distribution network and emerging markets. We're adding almost a dealer every day, while in the mature markets we're trying to shrink our dealer network. We

13

are going to add 1,300 dealers, and opening a dealer is a three-year process for us; recruiting them, making sure they're funded, getting approval for location, hiring all the people and getting them trained in their areas of expertise, whether its repairing or financing. It's a very long process. Adding 1,300 dealers is almost unprecedented.

Another component of that same growth equation is not just Brazil, India, Russia, and China, but it is now quickly moving to Indonesia and Vietnam. And we're now seeing entire raw populations turning into core consumers. What happens when you move into these markets is they require you to have local engineering and purchasing for the suppliers and then all of a sudden, because the labor source is cheap, they start to export like China is starting to do with cars now. Then they become a true global. This is just starting to happen in the car world. *They* are the growth, and hiring in engineering, in manufacturing and purchasing, not just contact and assembly workers.

I'd have to say the last change frontier for us has been, and will be, the emergence of social, virtual, and digital communications. In a lot of industries it's moving from a mere 3–5 percent of media buy, to a third of spending. That doesn't happen without reason. I can see in our organization a future scenario of a brand manager having a Labor Day program all week in Houston, Texas. And over the following weekend the data is sent to a location halfway around the world. The information would be worked up by a complete stranger, who may not even speak English, let alone Texan, and on Monday morning the marketing manager is going to wake up and find out all about his or her performance from Indian analytics. This is the future of communications—real time, real-world.

Raoul Quintero: At Maquet, we fix hearts for a living. In the medical equipment business there are also some very unique

14

challenges coming, not the least being the complete transformation of our customer base. Over two-thirds of cardiothoracic surgeons in the U.S. are now part of a hospital group; they are hospitalists, employees of the hospital, not self-employed as was the norm. So what does that mean? It means that where our customer was once the physician or surgeon who made the call on what was purchased for a procedure, the decision is now being made by someone else. The customer is now a hospital administrator who may have no clinical background at all. Make no mistake, hospitals are being evaluated on two variables: patient outcomes and cost containment. Patient outcomes matter, yet purchasing decisions can and are dictated by insurance companies or committees based on cost tables. Our customers have changed to the point that the financial, not the clinical, takes precedence.

In many environments this has brought about what I call the fall of the relationship. Our people, while clinically trained and experienced, are no longer allowed in certain areas of the hospital. Access is intentionally limited, and contact discouraged. The relationship between provider and customer is what has suffered. That same physician who used to see 20 patients a day, now as a hospitalist, must see 30 to 40 patients in the same timeframe to make the same amount of money he or she did five years ago.

Extend that out another 10 years, and the hospitals will own the practices with physicians having minor decision-making capabilities. That relationship will not survive. I believe hospital business and medical healthcare will be dictated no different from the way insurance healthcare is dictated right now—dollars and cents. It will be even tougher for the hospital itself in that in the future the hospital will have to be graded equal or better than competing institutions within the same city to be able to be reimbursed at a level it can make money on. They will literally bet it all on their performance every day.

The changes aren't just on the hospital side, though. They are on our side as well. In medical devices, the start-up companies that used to be so prevalent, where the principal had a big idea and it was one product, they would establish an entire organization around selling one product. Those days are gone. I think you'll find these start-up companies being capitalized by the big players, with the anticipation of if and when the product does pass FDA, they will be absorbed into the larger organization.

On the mature end of the product spectrum, if the product is good for 99.8 percent of the population, it now simply doesn't make sense for us to invest heavily to capture the other two tenths of a percent. And many technologies have matured to that level. R&D will drop, and broader applications of the same technology are what will drive growth if there is any for a lot of the players. In a nutshell, we have to be just as conservative as the provider side. No one will be exempt.

Chuck Sykes: Looking out into the future, Don, we're going to emerge into the world now being described as this new normal. And what is that going to look like? I'm really not sure. It's hard to put one finger on it. I do think that the world is going to be global, but global in a more integrated way—toward one global community. We're global today, but when you use the word, right now, you still think of separate distinct countries and separate, distinct peoples. But I really believe that we're moving ever closer toward a more homogeneous, global civilization or community. Now, I'm not saying that this will happen in my lifetime, but that's the path I see.

Think about the power of networks. Half of the world's population, today, this year, is now connected to the Internet. So you've got over 3 billion people connected via the Internet. One of the things I think we are experiencing is people are forming new subgroups because of the Internet—subnetworks, so to speak. People are going to start finding a closer affinity or allegiance with the people who are connected to their networks than the people in their own country. The connectivity is going to break down what we today perceive as kind of the boundaries or borders of countries. I don't know what impact that's going to have on us, but that speed, that connectivity and networking, and the accompanying virtualization are going to have an enormous impact on business.

Like you, I see a world where I think the productivity we will get out of our workforce is going to continue to increase, primarily through the very powerful communications systems we're putting in place. It's interesting, just amazing, really, what we can do with these tools. My IT guy told me the other day that in the next 10 years we're going to generate more computing capacity than we have in the last 30 years. That is the power that will drive the change that's coming.

From Organizational to Personal

This is a lot to consider: emerging markets becoming relevant, even entire social classes growing from a zero base; customer evolution, digital media, and social network dominance; a momentous global change curve that we all ride together. Our thanks to Messrs. Farley, Quintero, and Sykes. They carry truly unique perspectives.

You've begun to learn about this new era, this no-normal version of growth, change, and relationships. Take some time now to reflect on their observations and what they might mean to you personally. What are *your* "externals" that are shaping your organization? How is *your* customer base evolving? Do you see allegiance to networks supplanting national loyalties in the distant future? How distant? You now see the beginnings of the organizational impact of this new era. Stay with us. Read on to find out about what this new era is doing to all of us as people—its *personal* impact on how we will relate to ourselves and to each other.

CHAPTER 2

Personal Impact: Losing the Ability to Connect

This new era we've seen ushered in with the twenty-first century has taken quite a toll on every organization around the globe. Given all the change we've seen in the last 30 years, it stands to reason that we'll see the same thing again within only 6 or 8 more years; the cycle *will* accelerate. In Chapter 1 we discuss what we call no-normal events and dynamics and their impact on all of us collectively, but what about their impact on each of us individually? What about how they affect the lives of every one of us and how we live and interact? Let's take a look.

We Are All Connected

Technology has played the single largest role in this no-normal era. Indeed, it has transformed our very lives. We are all connected. As a way to start our look into technology and its impact on people, consider these facts:

- There are almost *5 billion* cell phones being used on the planet today.

- Those 5 billion phones sent and received 7 *trillion* text messages last year.
- There are 1.5 billion functioning televisions globally.
- There are 1 billion broadband subscriptions in place.
- As we write these words, six weeks into a new year, 50 million personal computers have been sold since New Year's Day.
- The first billion personal computers took 27 years to find their homes.
- The second billion PCs sold in only seven years.
- One billion PCs are in use around the world right now.

Wow! The effect of a few lines of data is staggering! Five billion cell phones on a planet with fewer than 7 billion people. This means that over 70 percent of us have cell phones (90 percent in North America), and in many places around the world more young people have cell phones than own books. Of those 5 billion cell phones, 1 billion are smartphones that have the computing power to integrate many other technologies. And 1 in 10 of us have a second, "secret" phone we don't tell our family about. Scary!

Just as explosive as cell phones has been the growth of television. One and one half billion TVs with a billion broadband subscriptions in place. Would you believe that there are *10 million* television channels feeding them? This growth in programming has almost doubled in the last two years. Ten *million* channels of programming operating 24 hours a day, 7 days a week. Incredible!

We're not judging. It's neither good nor bad; it just is. There is nothing inherently good or bad in the explosion of technology and its applications. It is the world in which we live, work, and play. Perhaps it makes sense now to think about where it all came from—the backstory that led up to all this.

The development of this technology paralleled our quest to manage information. Starting in the 1930s, massive advances were made with mechanical and electromechanical equipment that far outstripped our human ability to calculate information ourselves. From there, the era of electronics was born one piece at a time. Electromechanical technology gave way to vacuum tubes, which then in turn gave way to transistors. Transistors, and their miniaturization, allowed for integrated circuits. And the race was on.

There is a commonly accepted guide, called "Moore's Law," which states that the number of transistors that can inexpensively be put on a circuit board doubles every two years. This law is attributed to Gordon Moore, cofounder of Intel. He made this observation in 1965. It has held true.

Where will it all end? Those in the know believe that computing hardware capable of inexpensively matching the power of the human brain will be available in the 2020s. We will soon be able to buy the hardware to mimic our own organic computing capacity for under a thousand dollars.

Hardware, Software, Wetware

The term *wetware* is an abstraction used in the computer world to describe our central nervous system—our brain. We would like to extend this context of technology to beyond just hardware. Let's take a quick look at the early reasons behind software development and then spread a double coat of thought over how we've now come to interact with it and how the use of technology has become such an integral part of our everyday lives.

From the beginning, and still true today, the general purpose of software application has been to save time and increase productivity. From the individual efficiencies driving word processing, spreadsheets, scheduling or contact management programs to proprietary code for the organization-wide consolidation of previously inconceivable amounts of data, the development of software was designed to make our lives easier and more efficient. This new era has added a new role for technology's integration into our lives: *entertaining and connecting* us, not just helping us.

In terms of entertainment or media applications, at one time there were only radios, records, and going to the movies. That was the extent of the use of electronics to make our lives brighter. Radio was also used for mass communication, as were the news-reels that were shown between or before movies at the theater. Today, we still have radios, records, and movie theaters—and a bit more. Television, DVDs, Blu-ray, MP3, iPod, video, computer and Internet gaming, pay-per-view events, on-demand movies or series originating right in our own living room with instant access every second of every day. Media usage sits in stark contrast to its initial levels. Some 75 years ago we might have averaged less than an hour and a half of any day on records, radio, and movies. Less than 40 years ago babies began to spend two hours or more in front of the television every day, with that increasing over the decades to an average of seven or eight hours per day for those 8 to 18 years of age. Today the average media exposure is an astounding eleven hours out of every day.

We've just scratched the surface so far. Media is personally available to every one of us today. What can't your cell phone do? Instant global communication, high-resolution digital pho-tography, texting, e-mail, video calling, Internet access, global positioning and mapping. Cell phones do it all. And how have we integrated them into our lives? We might as well wire them directly into our brains (in fact, operationally we have). Most of us never use the on/off switch. We keep them on, and keep them on us. You will notice people using them in any conceivable setting, checking e-mail and texts when they're in line, while they're driv-ing, during work, or during vacation. We know of some who take a quick glance before getting out of bed in the morning or even during a shower, and we've heard cell phone calls originating from the next stall in the airport restroom.

And let's consider demographics. From adults who keep their e-mail going 24 hours a day or keep a phone on all hours of the night to know where their children are, to the 14-year-old in one research article who had averaged sending or receiving 27,000 texts per month. In middle school, high school, and even grade school, the setting today is one of several clusters of kids and young adults, each with his or her own digital connection and identity.

This brings us to the world of social media. As an Internet application, social media are really in their adolescence. Basically starting with Friendster in 2002, joined by Myspace in 2003 and the now public king of all social media, Facebook, in 2004, and Twitter in 2006, social media are now undeniably viral and can in no way be ignored. Of every minute now spent on the Internet, 25 percent of them are spent on social media. It's estimated that 102,000 man-years of member minutes were spent just communicating on Facebook last year. As we go to press, Facebook is closing in on 1 billion members worldwide. LinkedIn, Twitter, and YouTube add hundreds of millions more networked together, and there are dozens of narrowly focused networking sites from Advogato to Zooppa. We are *all* connected.

The Time-Technology Coefficient: Losing the Ability to Connect

It's a wonder that we still know how to talk to each other. Now let's put it all together. Do you recognize any of these scenarios? We participated in a webinar for a client this morning who told us that while on the call she had three screens active on her desk; one for e-mail, one for the project she's working on, and a third screen split in two with the market on top and social media on the bottom. She also had an iPhone next to it all (on "silent," she said, so it wouldn't interrupt). Another common scene might be the teenager doing homework on the family room couch, with the TV on low across the room, books and notebooks spread out on the coffee table, a laptop open with several screens up (the high school site for the assignment, Facebook, Google, and instant message conversations), all the while texting with three to five friends and taking or making the occasional short phone call. Sound familiar? A third vision might be a long row of treadmills and ellipticals in a hotel fitness center. It's 6 a.m., and every machine is in use. Every early bird exerciser has a set of earbuds plugged into either the machine they're sweating over or their iPod or iPhone or MP3 player. They're watching the machines' personal TV and listening to a song shuffle or an audio book. No one is unplugged. The hotel provides a full basket of disposable earbuds right alongside the antiseptic wipes, towels, and water cooler.

Not Rocket Science, *Brain* Science

Do any of these tales resonate with you? Do *all* of these scenes ring true? What do they all mean? We know that hardware and wetware are irrevocably intertwined. Not only do we enjoy our electronic companions ("I love my new phone."), but most would also agree that we now *need* them. We need this technology, and not just to satisfy some new techno-addiction. We need it to carry on everyday life in a no-normal, no-*service* economy.

A while back, Craig Lambert, *Harvard Magazine*'s deputy editor, coined the phrase *shadow work* to describe everything we now do for ourselves that was once done for us. Now, our smartphone can't help us fill up our tanks with gasoline, but it plans our trips for us. Where once a travel agent searched for the right flight, accommodations, car rental, and even entertainment, we now do it ourselves with our computers or phones. The customer-company interface with most organizations today is carried out online. Most companies make it very difficult to actually talk to anyone. And even when we do, the person we talk to most often is there just to instruct us how to access *their* system to make changes to our account, order new equipment, correct errors (ours and theirs), or to complete a survey on how satisfied we are with the company's *service*. Organizations have offloaded this work in many cases as a cost-cutting strategy. Our governments every year require us to put in billions of hours of online labor just in tax compliance. Someone else's backroom work is now *our* shadow work. Welcome to your personal no-normal.

There is no getting around the fact that we don't have the option to live without technology. We don't. But let's at least find out what we know. What is technology doing to us? We know through research that the type of multitasking we've been discussing is fatiguing, not refreshing. Many of us have given up our downtime in the interests of productivity—downtime that our brains need to learn, to create, to form longer-term memories. We know that being constantly and continuously connected often fosters an inability to focus, to concentrate. We have no desire to argue fact or fiction when it comes to the effectiveness of multitasking. What we do know is that in a no-normal world, our mental dependence on technology plays directly into the way our brains are wired—for better and especially for worse.

Let's face it. We are all, by nature, easily distracted. We've got two circuits wired into our brains: the direct circuit and the narrative circuit. According to the work of Daniel Gilbert, our brains are wired so that we've got one circuit in which we experience the world directly, without filters, from our five senses. With boredom, distraction, or just timing, we're also equipped with a narrative circuit that will kick in with a constant stream of thought—our inner voice—first in response to information we take in through our senses and then going off on every tangent imaginable. Our brains *love* distraction. They love jumping from one thought stream to another. In fact, Gilbert's work shows that in a no-normal world we are distracted, engaged in our narrative circuit, on average almost *half* our waking lives. No-normal technology and our brains are a match made in heaven!

Any time you find yourself in a conversation with someone, expect each of you to jump circuits and check out much sooner and more often than you might think. In our workshops we run an exercise in which we ask individuals to pair up and tell each other about their first sale or management job (depending on the workshop). We give each person a sheet of paper with the word *out* written on it. The instructions are simple: when you find your mind wandering as your partner speaks, hold up the paper and say, "out." In addition, if you believe that your partner isn't really listening, hold up the paper and cry, "out." Even if you are speaking and find your own thoughts on something other than what you are saying, yell "out." With hundreds and hundreds of examples to draw upon, the average connection is less than 30 to 60 seconds before someone checks out. Many of us can't hold our *own* attention, even when we're trying, for one full minute. Our brains are crazy for no-normal technology.

This integration of hardware and wetware comes at a cost. The more we connect electronically, the less we connect personally. We are losing the ability to connect with each other. This is not conjecture; this is fact.

Empathy: The Organic Connection

The important issue here is the loss of the *empathic connection* with those who matter to us. In disconnect, when we're "out," we lose awareness of others. Empathy is the direct identification with another person's situation, feelings, and motives. The empathy connection, the belief that you understand and acknowledge another person—that you not only viscerally understand but also *care*—organically exists between us, almost without our trying. Let's explore the magic of empathy, the balance of empathy and ego, the science of empathy, and how we know we're losing it.

Empathy:

The action of understanding, being aware of or sensitive to, and even vicariously experiencing the feelings, thoughts, and experience of another.

To understand empathy, think about what happens to you when you watch a heavy hit during a hockey game. How do you react—emotionally and even physiologically—when you channel surf and catch a mixed martial arts cage match or a blooper reel of skateboarders landing face first on the concrete? Do you cringe? Does your pulse quicken and your blood pressure rise? Do your muscles flex and tense up, and in some instances do you react so strongly that you have to shift position, stand up, remind yourself to breathe, and finally change the channel?

This is empathy. This is what we mean by understanding and being sensitive to the feelings, thoughts, and experiences of another person. This *action* of connecting with another human being is empathy. And it's not just brutality or another's pain that we connect to. Can you recall the scene in *Forrest Gump* in which Forrest (played by Tom Hanks) is standing over Jenny's grave, updating her on how "little Forrest" is doing? Can you recall the lump in your throat by the end of that conversation? That is empathy in action.

What do we know about empathy? From the evidence of several fields of scientific study, we know that humans are essentially *social* animals; just about everything we do is either in reaction to another or targeted to others. This starts early. Day-old babies are known to start crying at the sound of another baby's distress. Within the first months of life (some studies show in the range of

27

12 to 21 days), infants begin to mimic the expressions of others as a connecting mechanism; it's hardwired. Not only can they reflect the tone and sentiment of an expression (such as happiness or sadness), but babies can specifically mimic your actions, whether it's sticking your tongue out or opening your mouth wide in surprise. This simple mimicry is the genesis of more complex connections later in life. Somewhere around two years of age toddlers start to react with helping gestures in response to the distress of others.

These are *two-way* connections. At the simplest level, babies respond one to another. We won't go into all the science here, but what happens is that we continue to connect, naturally, throughout our lives. We know that we naturally connect with others both emotionally and physiologically and usually do so without trying. This basic connection of understanding and caring about another human being (notice I didn't say "agree with") is a prerequisite to understanding what drives another person's intentions and motivations, and this leads to effective social interaction. The paradox is that along with our explosive rise in *electronic* connectivity, there has been a decline in our *organic* connectivity. We've lost a lot of it already, and *that* alone is the most significant individualized impact of the no-normal world.

The Empathy Crash of 2000

Based on research with over 14,000 college students, we know that people today do *not* connect with each other as they did 30 years ago. They don't *understand* in the same way; they don't *care* in the same way. Through 30 years of studies reviewed by the University of Michigan's renowned Institute for Social Research, we know that empathy remained constant from the late 1970s on. Then, right around the turn of the century, it dropped—*it crashed by 40 percent*. To find out more, first-hand, we interviewed the woman who conducted the research. Read on to hear in her words what is happening to us all.

Dr. Sara Konrath is an assistant research professor, Research Center for Group Dynamics, Institute for Social Research, at the University of Michigan. Her groundbreaking work on empathy has been published in scholarly journals, magazines, and newspapers including the *New York Times, BusinessWeek,* and *USA Today.*

Bring Out the Best: Sara, thank you for joining us. What is your operational definition of empathy?

Sara Konrath: I really like your definition, it's very succinct—that someone understands and that they care. I distinguish just like you between the cognitive component of empathy being imagining another's perspective and then some level of not just understanding but *feeling* the emotions that they feel.

Bring Out the Best: You ache a little for them?

Sara Konrath: Yeah, you ache for them, because you feel it. Or you see their face, and there's a flicker of emotion, and you have that flicker in response. That's empathy.

Bring Out the Best: Right. And in terms of a summary around your research, tell us about how you got into it.

Sara Konrath: Well, for my dissertation project, I was actually studying the flipside: narcissism, or too much ego focus. I was looking at people with excessive self-focus—at nonclinical, everyday people, and how they score on the personality trait of narcissism, which we define as having an overinflated self-esteem, where their self-esteem is much higher than it should be given the circumstances.

Bring Out the Best: They probably aren't alone in that.

Sara Konrath: Yeah, that's what we found. We tracked narcissism over time in college students and found it had been increasing dramatically since the beginning of the study in the early 80s. I started shifting more toward studying empathy because in the data it seemed that higher narcissism was related to low empathy, and I wondered whether that was real. So we did the study on both kinds of empathy—the caring kind, and the cognitive kind—and we found they were dropping drastically, especially in the emotional arena. We did what's called a meta-analysis of over 70 studies and 14,000 students. We used American college students because we wanted to be sure we could compare the same population over a long period of time. We've since confirmed that the findings hold true for other demographics besides college students.

Bring Out the Best: I recall you said that the big empathy crash took place around the year 2000. Was it really that sudden?

Sara Konrath: Absolutely. There was a 48 percent decline in *empathic concern*, your "caring" quotient, and over 30 percent in understanding, in what we call *perspective taking*. The average was 40 percent overall, and the real change happened after the year 2000—from the year 2000 on.

Bring Out the Best: This may not be part of your study, but off the record, do you attribute it to any specific cause? Do you have a hypothesis even if it isn't validated yet?

Sara Konrath: You're right, we do have hypotheses, and we believe there are different levels of causality to consider. It starts by thinking of each of us within different contexts. There's the individual within the family, then within the community, and ultimately within a cultural or societal context. There's been change going on at each of these levels, and it's hard to know which one is the bigger factor. It doesn't really matter as they're quite related to each other. At a family level the most significant parallel changes are size and structure. Families are smaller, more complex in terms of second and third marriages, with different norms in terms of who does what. Parenting styles have shifted a lot as well. Kids may simply not have the same opportunity to practice their interactions that they once did. At the community level significant change is found first in the educational environment. The rise in the "self-esteem" movement is seen every day where self-esteem is valued over self-control. That may be related as well. Parents are more "involved" than ever, to say the least, and with this blanket approach of everyone getting an award and no one ever losing, it's no wonder that young people are fixated on self. At that same community level we can look at civic participation rates dropping to see the same disconnect. Robert Putnam has a great book out called *Bowling Alone*. His point is that we participate in bowling at higher levels than ever before in history. At the same time, membership in bowling leagues is lower than ever before; we're bowling alone. We do everything alone. When was the last time you remember someone just dropping by? In fact, I think it's now considered quite rude to do so.

Finally, at a cultural or societal level, your writings on media saturation and technological connectivity are in agreement with our hypotheses. Time is a finite resource. The more time we spend connected to media, the less time we spend connecting with others. I also believe that with reduced time together, we do less for each other. I like to say that, "caring is not abstract." It's concrete. It takes *action*.

Bring Out the Best: So what is going to happen? With losing the capacity to connect with others, are we doomed to living apart, even if we're under the same roof?

Sara Konrath: I like to leave that open, actually, because I think empathy is, to some extent, changeable. It responds to situations; it's *teachable*, and it's connected to results. It *matters* at the bottom line.

Bring Out the Best: Please tell us more about empathy being tied to results. Why does it matter?

Sara Konrath: Drawing on research on empathy in physicians, teachers, and professors. Physicians, for example, have the goal of needing their patients to follow their instructions and get better. There is ample research demonstrating that physicians who score higher on empathy have patients who more often do what they ask (take the medication as directed, conform to diet, etc.), and in the long term that leads to better health outcomes.

With teachers there is a similar literature finding that confirms that how teachers rate themselves and how others rate teachers in terms of empathy is related to objective student performance measures, even performance on multiple-choice tests. And again, I think that has to do with a sense of receptivity. A student who feels understood and cared for has openness to learning and motivation to relate to or connect with the teacher in some way.

Bring Out the Best: So there is a correlation between a higher empathy score and students' test scores?

Sara Konrath: Yeah, and the word *correlation* is important because there are correlations we don't know about as well. We can all go back to our days of being in school, and I don't know what your personal experience was, but there are still teachers I remember and think about often who made a difference in my life, and these are not the teachers who I thought were the most abstract and brilliant and should've received the Nobel Prize. They were people who cared deeply and taught me to deeply care as well.

Bring Out the Best: If you could tell a practicing manager one thing about empathy, what would you say?

Sara Konrath: I think I would ask them whether they'd be willing to consider the value of empathy in leadership. I would just leave it open and see if it's something that *they* would see as valuable. At some point people need to see for themselves the importance of it. It's deeply human and has to come from within, not just someone telling you to do it.

Bring Out the Best: Sara, thank you so much for sharing your unique background and passion for the human connection. Is there anything we forgot to ask?

Sara Konrath: Nothing at all. It's been very enjoyable for me as well. I definitely want to read your book for the sake of my own leadership and empathy skills. Thank *you*.

A continuous electronic flood of information, rapid repeated bursts of data from multiple sources is an accurate depiction of individual life in the no-normal era. Whether we break down days into micro-moments in order to make the most of our time or to kill it, our electronic companions are here to stay. Life is now expressed in 140 characters or less, captured in less than 60 seconds of video, or played out in gaming or mobile app experiences of 2.2 minutes or less! We are so connected now that we can't enjoy broadcast entertainment at home unless we DVR or TIVO the show, and then race through it by fast-forwarding the commercials. At work, one company's WebEx participants attending virtual workshops only manage to engage with the event at a 10 to 15 percent rate (yes, WebEx tracks how long the webinar is the active window on each participant's computer). For all of us while we're in the office around the world, our computers change active windows an average of 37 times every hour, *including those of us who have multiple screens going.*

We know what no-normal does to organizations, and we know what it does to individuals. Next come the implications for *leading* in a no-normal world. Join us.

CHAPTER 3

Bring Out the Best:
Leading in the Next Decade

W e started off this first section discussing the global dynamics of growth, change, and relationships in a no-normal world. The very nature of these forces has changed forever. We then moved on to the impact every one of us experiences on an always on, always connected planet. Hardware, software, and wetware are now inseparable. And empathy, the human connector, is the casualty.

Global: Personal and Professional

Let's now focus on the *professional* impact of this new era. If you are reading this book, you are responsible for the output of others; your profession is *leader*. And whether you know it or not, there is a storm coming.

If you look back 20 or 30 years, you'll recognize the first symptoms of the decline of institutional loyalty. With the adoption of rightsizing as a survival strategy, organizational loyalty to the employee became a thing of the past. We have members of our own extended families who worked for Fortune 100 companies starting in their late teens. They worked hard for 30-plus years, retired by the age of 50, and enjoyed their pension years in comfort. Those same people are now in their eighties and have given little thought to money ever since. All was taken care of for them: cash flow, medical, dental, optical for themselves and their families. Does anyone fit that description in your extended family? We're betting you're thinking of a parent, or even more likely a grandparent, because it doesn't happen anymore.

How many of *us* can retire at 50? How many companies can offer such comprehensive pensions and benefits? How many of us will work our entire careers for a single entity? Very, very few. The "greatest generation" example of one job–one career was supplanted by baby boomers who averaged 11 jobs between the ages of 18 and 44. Who knows where the averages will end up for generation X, generation Y, and beyond. The paradigm of frequent movement is alive and well. Organizations can no longer provide full support to a worker for 60 or 70 years in exchange for 30 or 35 years of service. The economics are not sustainable. Period. Pensions have been reduced, eliminated, or co-opted. Benefits have been drastically cut back, or cut out completely. The lifelong relationship between an organization and its employees is gone. On both sides.

Individual loyalty to the employer has taken the same hit. Loyalty in any relationship is *always* a two-way street. It doesn't matter which came first, the chicken or the egg. It doesn't matter who became disloyal first, the company or the employees. The net result is transience, and it's growing. Last year, an average of up to 55 percent of employees worldwide expressed a desire to leave their present employer. The number was only one in three in the United States, while over half of Brazil's workers desired a change in jobs. In either case, the number of employees expressing sentiments of loyalty to their employer, even in companies in the "best employer" category, is dropping fast. So why don't employees leave? Here is where the pressure is building. In a down economy you get economic hostages. Early in a no-normal world of lower headcount and higher productivity, there *is* nowhere else to go. There *are* no other jobs; people *can't* retire or quit. Pressure is building. Employees dissatisfied for any number of reasons want a change and can't make it happen. The talent exodus has yet to begin, but it will, and it's going to affect *you*.

Leading in the Next Decade

In preparing this chapter for you, we were fortunate enough to sit down with two of the world's most experienced and accomplished thought leaders in the area of leadership. Let's join them to discuss what's different in leading today from what it was 10 years ago, and what will be different 10 years into the future. Among the four of us we've got over a century of experience in the study and practice of leadership. It was quite a discussion. Let us introduce them.

First, Howard Morgan is the managing director of the Leadership Research Institute and specializes in executive coaching as a strategic change tool. He was named as one of the world's top 50 coaches, and Howard's profound understanding of the demands of leadership come from 17 years of experience as a line executive and executive vice president in industry and government.

The second is Marshall Goldsmith. Marshall is the million-selling author and editor of 33 books and was recently recognized as the number-one leadership thinker and number-seven business thinker in the world by the *Harvard Business Review*. His *New York Times* and *Wall Street Journal* bestsellers include *MOJO* and the *What Got You Here Won't Get You There* series. These have been translated into 28 languages. Marshall knows leadership.

Bring Out the Best: Thanks for being here, both of you. Let's roll into the first question. What *is* different about leading today from what it was 10 years ago, and what will change in the next 10?

Marshall Goldsmith: Globalization has become even more important than ever before. Understanding cross-cultural implications, being technologically savvy, building alliances and partnerships—all of these are critical variables right now. I'll also add something I call *"shared leadership"* that is not so much telling people what to do, but asking, listening, and learning from the people we lead. Many of us manage knowledge workers, and this type of leadership is becoming much more important living in a knowledge-based society.

I think these same five trends are only going to continue to strengthen. People are going to be under more pressure than ever before, technology is going to make the world move even more rapidly than it already has in the past, and you can't do it yourself. The leader is a learner in this context, as opposed to an expert. Guess what? In the future you won't know enough to be an expert.

Howard Morgan: Absolutely, it's a continuous evolution that started long ago. And it's going to constantly evolve. I agree with your no-normal idea, by the way. One of the things we may look back on in our rocking chairs 30 years from now is in essence that this no-normal world forced a higher quality of leadership than any other era in history. The reason I say that is that until people are forced to be in a situation where they have to deploy superb skills, they will always find a path of lesser resistance.

Large spans of control, shifting demographics, and geography are great for doing two things. One is weeding out the bad leaders, because they won't be able to do the job. The second thing is really finding out who the great leaders are. There are some great leaders who really weren't our superstars when they were individual contributors. So we have to change that dynamic and say someone who is a great performer may not be a great leader; we also have to say someone who may not be the best performer may be a phenomenal leader in the future.

Bring Out the Best: Howard, what other trends do you see affecting leading in the future? With unemployment high, productivity demands going even higher, pressure growing on economic hostages, loyalty on either side a distant memory, and demographics already shifting, what else is coming and what's the implication to the leader?

Howard Morgan: What's happening now perhaps is that our people have become more reluctant to say what's on their mind, to ask for feedback, more reluctant to push anything that may have a negative backlash. You have people who have been around, some in their forties or fifties, and the net result is they're really looking at survival. Many have now gone underground or more "stealth" in what their real feelings are. If they can't guarantee themselves anonymity, they go dark. And as followers change, so do leaders. Becoming more comfortable ourselves with our people not speaking out, we might get more comfortable than is merited, and it just compounds.

Our people are hunkering down, and we go right under with them. We provide far less communication than might be needed. The "talent exodus" I mentioned earlier will come. At some point when people begin to feel better about the economy, there will be a chain reaction. You're going to find people leaving, and when they leave, so will some of their teams—a domino effect. It's like a perfect storm coming. All these factors coming into play at once. If we don't reengage our people, they're going to go in droves.

Bring Out the Best: Marshall, what is your current research telling you about engagement? Can we stop the exodus?

Marshall Goldsmith: Well, I'm working on some very exciting new research in the areas of employment and engagement with my daughter Kelly. She's a professor at the Kellogg School of Management, and her official name is Dr. Kelly Goldsmith. Anyways, we're working on employee engagement in a whole new way. We're focusing on teaching employees to engage themselves. So as opposed to, "What is the company doing to engage you?" we're really teaching people to focus on, "What can you do to engage yourself? How can you build your own engagement?" We've done studies with seven different companies, and the results we've had so far have been spectacular. I'm not suggesting that anything we've done in the past is wrong or inappropriate; I believe leaders need to do even more. The point is almost everything that's been done is only looking at half the equation: what the company or leader can do to engage you. It's *really* not focused on what you can do to engage yourself.

Bring Out the Best: In thinking along that line, what's in it for me as the employee to engage myself? Aren't they thinking, "Hey, it's your job to engage me."

Marshall Goldsmith: Well, let me tell you what's in it for you. On American Airlines alone I have over 10 million frequent flyer miles. One flight attendant is absolutely upbeat and positive, and one is negative, bitter, angry, and cynical. They are on the same plane, with the same company, at the same time, with the same pay, same uniform, and same employee engagement program. What's the difference? It's not what's on the outside. It's what's on the inside. Here's the payoff for the employee: On that three-hour flight when that employee is bitter, angry, and disengaged, the real loser is not American Airlines. This flight is one zillionth of the entire American Airlines business. This three-hour flight is not that significant. The real loser is not even the customer. The customer has largely written this whole thing off by now anyway and has very low expectations. The real loser is the flight attendant. Three hours of this human being's life have been spent being disengaged, bitter, angry, and disillusioned. The main reason to do it is that it's great for you! *It's your life!* If you are determined to be bitter, disengaged, and angry, knock yourself out! Nothing we do is going to help you.

Bring Out the Best: A lot of the "bitter," "disengaged," and "angry" reflects a pattern of habit. It's a buildup of factors that the employees may not be aware of, or maybe they haven't even mattered for a long time. You've told us yourself that overcoming inertia is key. Can you tell us more about that, and how to do it?

Marshall Goldsmith: Well, our default reaction to life is not to experience happiness, or to experience meaning, or to be engaged. Our default reaction to life is inertia. We all tend to go where we've been going and do what we've been doing and say what we've been saying. The power of inertia is incredibly strong, and it's not just big things—it's small things. I get off the airplane, go to the hotel room, and turn on the TV. Click. There's an idiotic made-for-TV movie about some cheerleader mother killing her daughter's friend. I spend two hours of my life watching this loser movie, and then after two hours I say, "Why did I do that?" I wake up the next morning, and I didn't get enough sleep. And I'm in a foul mood.

Well, why did I watch the movie? Inertia. We do what we've been doing, and we tend to do whatever is in front of us. Right? Whether it makes any sense or not. It's hard to break the power of inertia, and one of the things I believe in is measurement. If you measure yourself every day on how many minutes of TV you watched and how many hours you slept, you probably wouldn't watch the movie because you'd realize how stupid it is.

Bring Out the Best: So the metric is the mechanism to breaking inertia?

Marshall Goldsmith: Exactly. Ongoing metrics—not just a little bit of a metric, but a *very* frequent ongoing sense of measurement *and* a sense of awareness. It's very hard for us to maintain awareness of what we're doing. Doctor Atul Gawande at the Harvard Medical School wrote a great book called A *Checklist Manifesto.* In his book, he documents the power of a nurse asking the doctor a series of simple questions before surgery. The first question is, "Did you wash your hands?" Well, the results are amazing. When the nurse asks the doctor the questions, the odds of unneeded infection plummet, and the death rate because of unnecessary infection is cut by two-thirds. The huge majority of doctors in the United States don't have the nurse ask the doctor the question. Why? The ego of the doctor. Every week people die because somebody is too proud to be asked a question.

I talked to Dr. Gawande about this, and he said sometimes his nurse asks the question, "Did you wash your hands?" and the doctor's response may be, "I don't remember." He's an honest man! He's a brilliant man from Harvard Medical School, and he wrote the book. Sometimes *he* can't remember if he washed his hands five minute ago. It's not because he's stupid; it's because he's busy! How many days do we forget what's important? How many days do we forget to be happy? How many days do we forget the people we love? Constantly. Why? We're lost in inertia, and metrics help us find our way out.

Howard Morgan: In overcoming inertia, I also think it comes back to all the exercises the four of us have all done around management versus leadership. I think we're starting to see just how dramatically different they are. Management means I know what's going on. I'm almost a glorified project manager. Leadership is, how do I keep the people I want to keep? How do I give them what *they* want? Sometimes it's as simple as the praise and process you talk about. And do I give it to them at the pace they want?

That's how I overcome inertia. What we too often have are leaders who are uncertain because they are employees too, *and* they have the added burden of having to impact and influence outcomes for others. There is simply one answer to this leader's paradox: give yourself the freedom to *not* know all the answers. And if you have a boss who thinks you should have all the answers, I would start educating that boss, because sooner or later it's going to demoralize your people. As a leader overcoming inertia, I have to learn to let that go. And, you know what else? If you think about it, my challenge in the future will be to retain the core of my team. I'd say the goal will be three-quarters of my primary talent—to keep 75 percent of the team intact, motivated, engaged. Your title says it all. I'm going to have to bring out the best in my people and in myself to make that happen.

But it's not going to be easy. There are going to be several variables working against us. Look at our retiring workforce, and our non-retiring workforce. I was born and raised in Canada, and in my home province of British Columbia, they have basically eliminated retirement age. You said it yourself. Many simply can't retire, and in other industries, a critical mass will be leaving, not staying. You take the chemical industry; one company I can think of is going to lose 60 percent of its workforce in the next seven years. On one side we have the delicate mix of several generations, and on the other we're losing two-thirds of our organizational memory. The demographics are astounding! Throw on top of that the very real global dynamics of a virtual team, and we'll have leaders who barely know their team members. Think about that. Take a company like Apple that has more people outside the U.S. than in. You might only see your people two or three times a year.

Whether your personal challenge is losing talent to career maturity, trying to deploy a cadre with very little business acumen, a mix of the two, or simply trying to lead individuals you don't really know. This is the perfect storm we spoke of, and it's coming.

43

The success of our leadership will lie in how effective we are in deploying others, not in how effective we are in deploying ourselves. In a no-normal world your interaction is priority, not your knowledge. For leading in the future, it is engage or else.

Rules of Engagement

You've probably heard the term *rules of engagement* before. It is the name of a current television situation comedy. It was also the title of a movie starring Samuel L. Jackson and Tommy Lee Jones. But before that it was shortened in the armed forces to ROE. For those having served, it spells out *the appropriate actions for military personnel in the course of their duties.* This is what we will do for you: spell out the rules of engagement for leaders in the course of their duties. You've just heard the thoughts of two of the finest students of leadership alive today. *Interaction* is key, not your knowledge.

Engagement matters—how you can engage employees and how they can engage themselves. A leader's perfect storm is coming. Engage or else. Let's find out how.

In most circles, employees' engagement is defined in emotional terms; how they feel about their boss, the amount of trust and confidence they have in their leader, a reflection of their emotional attachment to their work. There are often measures of the probability employees will remain with the organization, the likelihood that they will make positive statements about their employer, and sometimes even tracking the level of discretionary effort one would expend in their work. In other words, lots of organizations already track employee sentiment and try to measure exactly how much "above and beyond" they go in what they do for a living.

But, what drives engagement?

1. Feedback and dialogue with the boss
2. The quality of working relationships
3. The perception that a leader lives the organization's values, not just recites them

Let's stop right here for a moment. There is a positive correlation, a known connection, between employee engagement—emotional attachment to our work—and bottom-line results. It is proven. It is fact. We are not going to hit you with a shotgun blast of data to prove the connection. As evidenced in our discussions with Marshall and Howard, employee engagement is highly correlated with effective leadership that tends to be associated with productivity and profitability. If you didn't believe that employees who care do better than those who don't care, you wouldn't buy this book. You wouldn't be reading this now.

Where is the rest of this book going to take us then? We're going to increase your odds of riding out the perfect storm of leadership that is just over the horizon, of coming out the other side intact and healthy. Stay with us. As you continue reading, you will:

○ Hear what your people want you to know, but have been reluctant to say to you
○ Receive the best of thousands of live suggestions on what to do to engage them
○ Learn how to target your efforts to retain this core 75 percent of your team
○ Own a behavioral model for organizing your interactions for engagement
○ Master the power of being present with others, to rescue dying empathy
○ Take home a protocol for leading in the moment and finding the energy to do it

These are big promises. We have big resources. Not only do we have the experience and expertise, we also have the access to experts regarding every aspect of what we promise. And we have answers. In the next two chapters, we'll give you the best of over 6,000 answers from around the world to four of the questions we should *all* be asking of our people:

1. If you could tell me *one thing* about my leadership of you, what would you say?
2. In leading you, what do you want me to *start* doing?
3. In leading you, what do you want me to *stop* doing?
4. In leading you, what do you want me to *continue* doing?

The answers, and the follow-up digging they inspired, are the basis for the *how-to* that follows in later chapters. Not theoretical. Factual. We asked the questions *for* you.

SECTION TWO

JUST ASK ME

Give yourself the freedom to *not* have all the answers, and understand that soon you won't know enough to be the expert. Learn how to ask and what to ask. Have the courage and confidence to ask and not tell. Find out what your employees want you to *know* and what they want you to *do*. This section contains the following:

- We asked *for* you. We took the initiative and surveyed what your people would say to you if they had the chance.
- We surveyed what they want you to stop doing, what you should start doing, and what you should continue doing as a leader; in every corner of the world and at every organizational level.
- We distilled thousands of survey responses, turned data into information, and information into knowledge that you can use right now. Read on.

CHAPTER 4

Just One Thing: What Your People Want You to Know

FIGURE 4.1   What Your People Want You to Know

No-normal leadership is all about asking. Not telling, *asking.* Think back to Chapter 2 for a moment; what did you hear from the top leadership minds of our day? It comes down to allowing old paradigms to die their natural deaths. Leader as cop, the long antiquated belief that the job of leaders is simply to police the performance of their people no longer applies. Leader as coach, the ultimate expert that functionally trains and maintains the technical competency and interactions of the team, no longer does it. These are not enough.

While remnants of these approaches are needed to varying degrees in many organizations, a new era requires a new view. Leader as engager—as enabler—is the role that will successfully navigate the perfect storm facing us all. Securing and maintaining the connection between the organization and the individual is our new role, and like our no-normal economy, that role hasn't been able to gel yet. We don't know for certain what is coming and what will be required of us. We don't know enough to predict or control, if we ever really did. If we don't know, we will have to find out. To find out, we will have to ask. We have begun the process.

Survey Background:
Who, Where, How, When, and What

Common sense tells us that asking works. As our friend Marshall mentioned, your people already know more than you about their role, their work, their reality on the job. You can't tell them what you don't know. Simply put, asking makes us more successful at influencing others. Those who ask how they can be more effective, adopt the suggestions they can, and follow through on resolutions for change see all their results improve. That is a fact. Let us describe what we've done for you in researching this book.

Who

We received survey data from more than 1,700 of our clients' employees around the world. Four companies are represented in the database. All responses were confidential and were sent directly to us. Complete anonymity was ensured. The organizational roles represented span the entire hierarchy (see Figure 4.2). The largest single group of respondents, at some 54.2 percent, as you would expect, comes from the ranks of "individual contributors." People with a manager title, but no direct reports, make up 10.1 percent

FIGURE 4.2   Professional Role of Survey Respondents

Individual contributor			54.2%
Manager (no reports)			10.1%
Manager (direct reports)			24.6%
Manager of managers			5.4%
Director			3.9%
Executive			1.7%

of the responses. Managers *with* direct reports represent 24.6 percent of all responses, and managers of managers, directors, and executives make up 5.4, 3.9, and 1.7 percent, respectively.

Along with knowing the organizational role they fulfill, a second demographic question gave us validation as to whether or not we tapped into the needs of *everyone* surveyed from the perspective of tenure—that is, their level of professional experience (see Figure 4.3). The largest group of respondents, 37.8 percent, had 5 years or less of professional working experience in any organization (not just their current employer). Almost 30 percent (29.4) had between 5 and 10 years of working experience, 12.3 percent had been part of the workforce for 10 to 15 years, and 20 percent have

FIGURE 4.3   Professional Experience of Survey Respondents

5 years or less			37.8%
5–10 years			29.4%
10–15 years			12.3%
More than 10 years			20.5%

over 15 years of working experience of one kind or another. When compared to the overall demographics of our four client organizations, this spread very accurately reflects the levels of business acumen or professional maturity across their ranks.

Where

Our survey responses originated just about equally from every corner of the planet. We asked a third and final demographic question requesting that respondents indicate the global region in which they work (see Figure 4.4). Asia-Pacific (APAC), Latin America (LATAMS), and North America were almost exactly level in representation at 28.7 percent, 27.9 percent, and 27.3 percent, respectively. Europe-Middle East-Africa (EMEA) showed the least representation at 16.1 percent. These levels of participation again accurately reflect our client organizations' personnel distribution throughout the world.

What

We chose our questions carefully. From a wealth of personal experience and related research, we know that personal and relational change and effectiveness are never easy, but they had better be simple. We used to ask our coaching clients to select up to three areas of focus for change or personal improvement. The longer we've been at it, the clearer it has become that the ideal number of

FIGURE 4.4 **Geographic Region of Survey Respondents**

APAC		28.7%
EMEA		16.1%
LATAMS		27.9%
North America		27.3%

operational or behavioral change initiatives for *anyone* is one. Not three, not two, but *one*. That's why in the first question we asked, respondents had to limit their feedback to just one thing they would like to tell their boss about his or her leadership of them.

Here is another bit of background that drove the crafting of the questions we asked in preparing for this book. The single driving enabler of change for successful people is that what they choose to do differently be self-selected. This means that the change you might want to take on is your idea, your priority, your change, not someone else's. Our objective was to give you options so that any change that results a few hundred pages from now is your idea, your choice. We settled on the convention of *stop-start-continue* in that it lends itself to simplicity; it runs the gamut of what is not working, includes what might work and what is already working for you. This leaves room for choice. The four questions we asked were:

1. If you could tell your boss *just one thing* about his or her leadership of you, what would you say?
2. In leading you, what do you want your boss to *start* doing?
3. In leading you, what do you want your boss to *stop* doing?
4. In leading you, what do you want your boss to *continue* doing?

How and When

You know *who* gave us answers for you and *where* they live and work. *How* we asked our questions was via electronic means: e-mail and intranet web postings. The context of our questions—that of background research for a professional text—was transparent. We informed participants *why* we were asking the questions. The questions were asked in some cases within six months of this book's publication date (meaning that the research is current and relevant). We asked our questions of people just like you and yours, from an organization much like yours, in the same part of the world where you live, and at a level of experience and authority much like yours. In this respect, these answers may be much like what yours would be.

Survey Analysis: How We Distilled Meaning from Data

We received responses from nearly 1,700 people to four questions (not including demographic questions), which gave us approximately 7,000 written responses. These were not multiple-choice questions; they were open-ended. Some responses were short and sweet, while others went on and on. We ended up with tens of thousands of words of feedback and suggestions. You can imagine the difficulty of perceiving patterns in the wealth of information we received. How did we do it? *Text analytics.*

Text analytics applies computer software (fighting fire with fire) to linguistic techniques in order to extract meaning from content. We've long been accustomed to business intelligence applying technology to crunching numbers, and within the last 10 years we've developed the technology to crunch text. In a nutshell, text analytics can detect patterns, relationships, and even sentiment in any large body of text. We can now efficiently, reliably, and easily determine how often words come up, how words pair up, and even the *emotion* behind the use of the word groupings. For several hundred years people have attempted to do the same thing, but manually—culling and clipping newspaper articles and trying to visually interpret meaning. In a no-normal world the computer does it for us—faster, better, and more cheaply. Today, we're betting that many of you have seen text analytics output—on Facebook. If you've heard the term *word cloud,* that's text analytics. It uses font size and grey scale to visually portray the frequency and sentiment of the words used in any survey or collection of words (like

Facebook posts over a period of time). Impressive stuff, and we're bringing it to you here.

The second method of analysis, *verbatim review*, is a 50-cent way of saying that we read and sifted through every one of the 7,000 responses. In other words, we used old-fashioned subjective human interpretation of what we received. That too is the authors' job, and we were happy to do it for you. What comes next is what we found out, through technology and traditional review, about what your people want you to know about leading them.

Survey Findings:
What Your People Want You to Know

Let's start by asking a question of *you*. The first of the four survey questions was: *If you could tell your boss just one thing about his or her leadership of you, what would you say?* What would you guess was the incidence of purely negative responses? We don't mean constructive criticism. We mean negative evaluations. Take a second to think about it. Most people we ask this of assume that anywhere from 50 to 80 percent of the responses would be highly negative. In reality, only 7 percent of the responses were completely negative.

Would you care to venture another guess as to the number-one response to this question? Almost 1,700 people were asked what they would say if they could tell their bosses just one thing about their leadership, and the top answer was, "Thank you."

The second most frequent response? "Well done" or a mix of *appreciation* and *acknowledgment* for a job well done. Phrases that begin with "good," "great," and "excellent" after a simple thank you were usually part of the second most frequent responses.

The word cloud (see Figure 4.1) at the beginning of this chapter depicts the responses to: "If you could tell your boss just one thing, . . ." The larger the letters are displayed, the more *frequent* the response, and the darker the letters are represented, the more *positive* the sentiments behind the comment. Take a very long look to see for yourself in one powerful visual what your team would tell you if it could.

In this case, a picture is worth many thousands of words. What do *you* see? We've provided the background, the method, and now the findings. What are your impressions, observations, and conclusions about what you see? We provide our own thoughts about the data in later chapters. At that time we help you get organized and set up your own protocol for effective leadership in a no-normal world. Right now, we want you to take in and consider the honest feedback of 1,700 people very much like your own team members.

And, here is another way to portray the sentiment expressed within the words of the survey results. It's called a *category leaf report,* or more simply put, a pie chart of the basic emotions expressed (see Figure 4.5). Take a look again for yourself. It represents the emotional spring-load of your people in answering the question, *If you could tell your boss just one thing. . . .* Surprising, isn't it? One observation we will share with you is that in our view you do *not* lead an angry, disaffected workforce. If you were to believe only what you see and hear on TV, the Internet, or your local newspaper, you would think that the entire world was angry, demotivated, and disengaged. This is not true, at least not in the

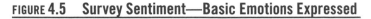

FIGURE 4.5   Survey Sentiment—Basic Emotions Expressed

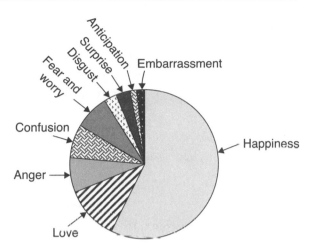

organizational setting. What you're hearing are the people with the microphones. In our opinion, the majority of your people, the *core* of your team, is waiting to be engaged. They are waiting to be asked, and the data support us.

We've edited the dozens and dozens of "thank yous" and "good jobs." What follows are many of the verbatim responses we found to be representative, meaningful, useful, and informative. We have sorted them by the major categories that the text analytics gave us: communication, praise and recognition, treatment and respect, feedback, and independence. We've done the heavy lifting for you. Now, enjoy listening to the voice of your team.

For all categories, the question was: If you could tell your boss just one thing about his or her leadership of you, what would you say?

Communication

"If I knew what you were working toward, then I could spot more opportunities." / "Always be positive." / "You're approachable but

not encouraging. There is a difference." / "Be aware of body language and of your own behavior. You can have respect for people in your words, but they mean nothing if the respect is not given in your nonverbal language." / "Have a positive disposition—always—even during uncontrollable, unavoidable, unmanageable situations." / "Follow the chain of communication." / "Bottom-up prioritization is just as important as top-down." / "Don't hoard the information we need to do our job." / "Don't lead through e-mails—talk." / "Don't send coaching e-mails to the whole team when only one of your reports is the problem." / "Stay in touch with your human side." / "I like that your actions are a reflection of your words." / "I would tell you to be present." / "A leader inspires." / "It would be nice if you could look me in the eye." / "Leadership means the capacity to engage, represent, and motivate others to become the best they can be." / "Make contact with your 'team' more often." / "You know how to separate friendship from work." / "Please don't send generic e-mails to the team about not following procedures. It's offensive for those who are dedicated and do actually adhere to procedures." / "People with no people skills should not lead or attempt to do so." / "Listen more; talk less." / "You lead by example. You are a good listener." / "I have not spoken to you in nearly two months." / "Be passionate; be patient." / "Commitment and communication." / "I wish your actions were a reflection of your words." / "Start being present and genuine during conversations. Unless someone is bleeding, put the damn phone away." / "Stop trying to impress me." / "Continue to share that vision with me. Thank you. That sharing (good or bad) means more than you know." / "Start involving me earlier." / "I appreciate and honor the open, honest, and candid way you express yourself and communicate." / "Remember, your words in e-mails show no emotion. I don't know how you feel." / "You have to ask to find out what is important to me." / "Speak with behavior, not just words." / "Stop saying thank-you; start doing thank-you."

Praise and Recognition

"You're doing a great job." / "Motivation and support!" / "Acknowledge the people you've asked a favor of." / "Remember that even the brightest of smiles can hide the darkest of thoughts." / "Always remember to care for your subordinates, and thank them." / "Thanks for standing up for your employees." / "If I do well and exceed all targets, please compliment me and then ask how I do it." / "Don't assume that I don't need praise. I do." / "You are the most patient and calm person I've ever met." / "I just realized that I am not yet capable of having your position." / "I couldn't do what you do every day. Keep it up!" / "I wish I'd had a boss like you two years ago." / "Thank you for caring!!" / "I would tell her that she is doing a great job." / "If it weren't for you, I'd have given up a long time ago." / "You are someone I want to follow, not a boss I have to follow." / "I'm doing fine, but thanks too for asking." / "I appreciate that you want to make sure I understand, but ask me instead." / "Praise and reprimand right on the spot. Thank you." / "Really care for your people and they will care about the work." / "Positive comments are just as important as constructive comments." / "She is fair and honest; it's hard to find a leader that is both!" / "You do an awesome job, and you do not get told enough!" / "You are strict—but cool!" / "You are an employee many companies would love to have." / "I love what I do!"

Treatment and Respect

"Have faith in your team!" / "A happy boss promotes a happy team." / "Less flinging stuff around. A monkey could do it better than you." [Authors' note: Sorry, we had to leave that one in. It's too good not to include.] / "Ask the question now if you know you're going to need a well-developed answer later." / "Be fair and not a plonker." / "Don't forget about me—perhaps I can help." / "Fulfill the promises you make to the team; I support you." / "Be aware how the small workers sometimes feel." / "Good leadership starts with knowing the names of your direct reports." / "Ensure your team feels they are being led, not just managed." / "We are essential to the company, but forgotten." / "I can accept reprimands but not in front of my coworkers." / "I lead others as you lead me." / "I like that he knows my name and greets me with a smile every time he sees me." / "I need to feel that you are my boss and not just a person between me and the director." / "There is no excuse to leave me aside." / "It is very easy to make the rules when you don't have to follow them. It's also easy to throw out an answer when you have no idea what the problem is." / "Don't forget that we are just like you." / "I'm doing fine, but thanks too for asking." / "Don't take advantage of those who are dedicated by just expecting them to accept." / "People respect you more when you are not just trying to please everyone." / "You are a servant leader, but too much service will make the team dependent on you and therefore helpless." / "Just because I'm over 50, doesn't mean I'm stupid." / "Do not mix personal and professional." / "The measure of a successful leader is the success of their employees." / "There is a reason why it is called leadership and not 'bossing around.'" / "Treat me as a person, not a statistic." / "Treat your employees the way you would like to be treated." / "We are in the same ship, what is good for you must be good for me; what is good for me must be good for you." / "Don't treat us like you don't want us." / "Not anger—answers!" / "Take care of me so you don't lose me." / "Without followers you have no job."

Performance Review

"Thank you for your feedback in real time." / "All company layers need coaching." / "Analysis of numbers, data, and information is key to success today. Relationships are needed to grow tomorrow." / "Ask me: What are my goals, my aspirations?" / "I like assertive—my boss clearly states what is expected; there are no misunderstandings, and we get the desired results." / "Be a good manager and not my brother or friend." / "You haven't put in a day's work until you've taught someone else something new." / "Be with us on the battle field." / "Commitment is the basis of success!" / "Thank you for sometimes changing your schedule to meet our needs instead of us changing ours to meet yours." / "Expectations should not be set so low or so high that employees feel powerless in shaping their future." / "I appreciate all the guidance. I appreciate the structure." / "You are consistent, supportive, open, and trustworthy—all traits vitally important to a successful working relationship." / "I know I am your friend, but, hey, you are also my boss! Stop treating me different, and start helping me improve!" / "I need you to be honest with me and not always worry about hurting my feelings." / "Don't take sides just because you like someone; check the results." / "Thank you for taking me out of my comfort zone." / "I've learned so much, but I need to grow some more." / "Just be fair (this generates loyalty; loyalty generates commitment)." / "Make time to understand what drives me, and then lead to that." / "My boss has this unique way of stretching my capabilities without my feeling it." / "I also feel my boss is like a babysitter to a lot of the employees. Who are you hiring?" / "Leaders make other people produce their best, either as individuals or collectively." / "A leader is a person who takes action, either directly or by encouraging and directing others." / "Stop for a minute. Breathe. And think of the volume of tasks you have delegated first before adding to the pile." / "I never have mistakes. I have learning opportunities." / "There is a difference between developing someone and burning them out." / "Give me daily feedback on my performance, not just the formal one." / "Develop people—trust us to get the job done." / "Become involved with the people you lead." / "I greatly appreciate that you don't load me down so that I can spend more time out in my territory getting my job done." / "Perfect, I can't be that." / "I'm not perfect for the job, but I am trying." / "I appreciate your wanting to make sure I understand, but try asking instead of just telling in another way." / "Show me the way, and I will follow." / "I'm not your PDA." / "The boss knows how it's done; the leader shows how it's done."

Independence

"A career is more than just a role to be filled, more than a job." / "We often hear about the future of the company, but that future is my future—several thousand voices at a time." / "Allow us to do our job." / "At times we do need to be told what to do, and at other times we want to be fully included in the process. Your challenge as a leader is to work out which and when." / "Take it easy when you are concerned about something. I might have already taken action to address it." / "Be more patient with me." / "Delegate more of your workload— I can help." / "I sometimes like the hands-off style, but its leaves me wondering if I'm doing things right or the way you want them done." / "Trust me that I will make you look good." / "I appreciate that you don't micromanage me and allow me to work independently." / "It may be time to reevaluate the weaker members of the team." / "I'd tell you two things: refrain from being impulsive, and learn how to trust your people." / "Trusting your people by giving them a sense of accountability." / "I am very proud to be someone who she can rely on." / "Leadership is not equated with one's position, although it is most likely required from those who are in the position." / "Lead me, but don't control me." / "Put me in front of your boss more frequently, so I can live in your shoes." / "Thank you for trusting me." / "He believes in me, and as a result makes me believe in myself." / "I appreciate your letting me do my job and take ownership." / "If you treat people as if they can't be trusted, you'll only attract the untrustworthy." / "No excuse not to use me." / "Continue giving me autonomy and the ability to make decisions without layers of approval. Thank you." / "You hired me because you thought I could do the job. Now let me do it." / "Thank you for trusting me to manage myself."

These responses set your head spinning, don't they? The good, the not so good, the inspiring, the honest. What you've just experienced is a fire hose dose of sincere feedback. Let's close the chapter now with a bonus. We asked a few of our interview subjects what they would say if they could tell our readers *just one thing* about leadership.

Jim Farley (group vice president, global marketing, sales and service, Ford Motor Company): The one thing I would say is learn a lot more about Bobby Knight. In the future a lot of us are going to be Bobby Knight or Tony La Russo. Some coaches seem to craft not just athletes, but great young men and women. Why? Because some coaches can connect them to a higher calling, work on their technical expertise, engage them emotionally, and get the most out of the average player. Lasting success isn't built on the superstar.

Raoul Quintero (president and CEO, U.S. sales and service, Maquet Medical Systems): I would tell them to forget about status quo. There is no such thing. Lead through change.

Chuck Sykes (president and CEO, Sykes Enterprises): Just the old words of wisdom I heard a long time ago: do right and right will follow. Whatever you are faced with, and you will be faced with a lot very soon, just do the right thing. You'll know what it is.

Marshall Goldsmith (author, speaker, and coach): I would tell your readers perhaps three things about leadership in a no-normal world. Have the courage to ask for input and look in the mirror. Have the humility to admit you can improve, and have the discipline to follow up and get better.

Howard Morgan (author, coach and managing director of the Leadership Research Institute): Recognize that the success of your leadership lies in how effective you are in deploying others; it's no longer about how effective you are in deploying yourself. Let go and let good people do good things.

CHAPTER 5

Six Thousand Insights: What Your People Want You to Do

FIGURE 5.1   What Your People Want You to Do

You've studied what your team members want you to know, and what a powerful message that is. Now you can find what they want you to *do*.

Our friend Marshall Goldsmith is fond of saying, "What is less important is your understanding of the practice of leadership. What matters most is *practicing* that understanding of leadership."

Knowing is one thing. *Doing* is another. With literally thousands of speaking and training participants over the years, we often stop early in the process and ask them to comply with a simple request.

What seems like a trick is only mixing signals a bit. In a room of hundreds, we ask them very plainly and calmly to make a fist and place the fist on their chin. The somewhat mixed signal we give is that while we *say* the word "chin," we place our own fist on our cheek. We've given the instructions very clearly, but we've contradicted them with our behavior. Can you guess which instruction they invariably follow? Where do they place their fist? On their *cheek*, of course. *People respond to what we do*, not to what we know. They barely listen to what we say. Knowing might help *us* understand and accept, but what we *do* is what impacts others. What we *do* influences how others respond to us. Let's find out now what your team wants you to *do*.

Five Plus or Minus Two

There's a classic learning theory that says that we can best remember information in groupings of "five plus or minus two." Have you ever noticed that phone numbers and credit card numbers limit each grouping to a maximum of four numbers? It's done for a reason; it makes it possible for us to *remember* them. We're going to do the same for you. We've collected several thousands of suggestions from around the world on what we all want our bosses to start, stop, and continue doing when leading us. Through text analytics we can extract the frequency and sentiment of word usage. That same text analysis has also grouped them by frequency in the categories of communication, praise and recognition, treatment and respect, performance review, and independence. Like many of the more powerful truths you'll come across in this lifetime, it's simple, but not easy. It's very simple to understand, yet often very difficult to make happen in practice. Let's tackle simple first.

In our survey database we have thousands of responses to a few basic questions about what we want our leaders to do. The responses are relevant, timely, and equally represent every organizational level and tenure within each geographic region on earth. That is simple; that is fact. Through mature text analytics we have run category reports that classify these responses according to subject areas. This too is simple; this too is fact. We can tell you that in each report we've run, these five categories are the ones that matter to your people. The five-plus-or-minus-two critical success factors to connecting with members of your team, to effectively leading them in a no-normal era, come down to communication, praise and recognition, treatment and respect, performance review, and independence.

Now comes the *but not easy* part. As you review the "stop/start/continue" verbatim responses coming up, you too are going to be getting some mixed messages. In one response you'll hear, "Talk to me more, and not just through e-mail," while in the very next response you might hear, "Be silent for once." One time it's "Ask for my opinion," while another it's "Tell me what *you* want." Simple, but not easy. There is no single response to address every person or every situation, but there are rules. What you have now are the beginnings of what we call the rules of engagement.

With this framework in mind then, let's review the raw responses we thought would be meaningful for you. Again, we've done the heavy lifting. What follows is what to stop, what to start, and what to continue. As you read the survey responses, think in terms of where each might fall—communication, praise and recognition, treatment and respect, performance review, or independence. We believe you'll find certain responses that personally resonate with you, either at work or at home. Take a deep breath. Soak it all in.

Survey Questions and Responses

The survey questions and the verbatim responses are all listed below, but let's start with the big picture. The word cloud in

FIGURE 5.2 What Do You Want Your Boss to Start Doing?

Figure 5.2 shows a visualization of the responses to the question, What do you want your boss to *start* doing?

Note the frequency and prominence of "give feedback" and "provide feedback." Both of these touch upon the feedback categories of praise and recognition *and* performance review (there are two sides to the feedback coin—praise and process). Many of the others you see will represent greater or lesser degrees of other categories, and each descriptor you see can also represent more than one category at the same time (for example, "feedback" can represent both praise and recognition as well as communication). In viewing the word cloud, go with your impressions. It is meant to create a visual synopsis for you. Take them in as a single image. You will get the details soon enough.

The second big picture has everything to do with sentiment. What some companies call a leaf report we call the "sentiment pie," which is a pie chart of the emotions represented (see Figure 5.3) in answers to the question, *What do you want your boss to* start *doing?*

The sentiments that come up relate to happiness, confusion, anger, and fear and worry, yet the overriding emotion is all about happiness. Even when we ask what the leader should start doing, it is still a very happy pie. Again, take away a general impression of what you see, and don't overanalyze. Make a mental note of your

FIGURE 5.3   Start Doing—Basic Emotions Expressed

impressions in viewing the frequency and sentiment expressed by a couple of thousand responses to what your people want you to *start* doing in leading them—feedback, communication, happiness, confusion. Leave these as advance organizers. Now take a highlighter and some uninterrupted time to read through the verbatim responses. Mark up the responses that resonate for you.

Survey Question 2: What do you want your boss to *start* doing?

"A daily touch." / "A good conversation." / "Acknowledging accomplishments." / "Acknowledging the efforts of your team." / "Providing me with feedback and not waiting until my yearly review." / "Delegating some of your workload to give me the exposure that I need to help you." / "Being more relaxed." / "Talking to me not just through e-mail." / "Allowing me to give opinions without stopping me before I even start." / "Asking for suggestions." / "Asking for my opinion." / "Asking me how I am and not just how can I improve."

"Being a decision maker, not a follower." / "Being a role model first—leaders model what they want." / "Being an example to those

down the line." / "Being as simple as possible and to the point." / "Being available." / "Being honest, kind, and polite when it comes to performance observations." / "Being knowledgeable about what your staff can do along with their limitations."

"Trying to listen and not just pretending to listen." / "Being more involved with your team." / "Being more relentless in trying to get things changed." / "Being specific in your communication. I like knowing what the details are." / "Just because you know what you want it to look like doesn't make me a mind reader." / "Sharing— it's frustrating to do the task three times because you had a vision in your mind that you didn't bother to share." / "Communicating; being specific." / "Being specific, transparent, and fair."

"Being straightforward; giving immediate feedback." / "Recognizing me when my work has exceeded what was expected of me." / "Being more specific in what is needed from me." / "Being more transparent when pushing ideas down from the next level." / "Building mutual trust between us." / "Calling me out on specific behaviors that you think I can do better on." / "Communicating a desired outcome, with specifics about what you expect in an end result." / "Communicating with me. Don't assume I know what I am doing; make sure."

"Communicating—meaning two things: (1) listening when I speak and (2) giving meaningful feedback and information to help me do my job." / "Considering all those things that are not visible in the statistics." / "Correcting me as soon as I make a mistake. Don't wait." / "Designing an incentive structure that is based on what drives me." / "Not allowing a previous incident to effect a current decision." / "Don't just tell me to do something; start showing me how to fix it!"

"Ensuring that we get a little more than just the minimum out of all of us." / "Explaining to me the why of a situation so that I can understand." / "Delegating more responsibility. I would like for you to trust that I can also complete some of the tasks." / "Facing me with a smile." / "Focusing and listening to my concerns." / "Being clear, precise, and open." / "Following through without reminders from me." / "Gaining my trust." / "Providing clear and direct guidance. Don't keep me guessing." / "Giving clear but concise instructions." / "With daily feedback." / "Giving me feedback and coaching. You've never done so." / "Giving me more authority to make a decision and either trust in my ability to do so, or go back to directing me." / "Giving me more authority to make my own decisions—especially after success has trumped failure."

"Greeting me. Say hi with a big smile." / "Guiding me every step of the way—until I'm on my own." / "Guiding me to get results, not just demanding them." / "Having a heart." / "Congratulating what I've done. After that you can tell me what I need to grow." / "Holding team meetings with your direct reports, rather than managing us one off."

"I would really like to have a meeting with you once a month or every two months so we can take time to talk about what I do right or wrong." / "I know the question is about 'me,' but I need to be a part of a cohesive team that can collaborate and survive healthy conflict. Start bringing the team together so we can develop a plan to address business opportunities and challenges." / "I know it's due to a lot of responsibility, but I would like to start seeing you more often." / "I need to feel that my work counts, that I'm a valuable asset in the team."

"I want her to start talking to each of us once a month." / "Giving examples first, before asking me to do a task that I am not familiar with." / "Explaining things in a simple way and not just by the book." / "I want to be challenged." / "Asking me to do more 'planning ahead' with you." / "Taking your time when you need to explain issues." / "Involving me more, especially in decision making that involves my team." / "Jumping off a cliff." [Authors' note: We didn't say there were no negatives.] / "Leading me with support and clear boundaries." / "Keeping me in the loop on your work, so I am

71

aware of organizational successes and struggles and can even offer assistance." / "Knowing my expectations and to use them as a guide to understand me."

"Learning what it takes to do what you assign others to do." / "Giving the must-know processes and where to find information." / "Listening, before saying anything." / "Listening to the entire question before trying to answer." / "Stopping the 'macro' managing—find out what I do." / "Making me do my best each day." / "Making me feel supported, despite the challenges in front of me." / "Meeting the human being in me first." / "Holding more structured one-on-one meetings." / "Other than having more one-on-one time, there really is nothing else that I can think of. You are doing great." / "Providing coaching and guidance for growth." / "Providing constructive feedback."

"Providing feedback on my work and my value to the company." / "Providing performance feedback one on one." / "Providing more precise details." / "Providing specific expectations, and reviewing my progress against them."

"As you climb the ladder, I often hear that objectives become less clear, more ambiguous. I disagree. If the CEO can set clear expectations for Wall Street, then every manager can set clear expectations within the organization." / "Putting trust in me until I show that I can't be trusted. If the default status is lack of trust, then what possible good can I do?"

"Public recognition is the best incentive." / "Separating work from personal biases." / "Having vision, being visible." / "Spending more time one on one with me." / "Getting to know me." / "Setting realistic metrics or goals. I'm not a robot." / "Starting by being more friendly." / "Starting out with a positive." / "Start teaching; don't be a fault finder." / "Building the relationship." / "Start trusting me and my abilities."

"Starting with a smile; you'd be surprised." / "Starting to see me as a human being and not as a number, or worse." / "Taking *ownership of your leadership role." / "Taking us away from the pod; what you tell us individually is nobody else's business." / "Communicating with me on a daily basis." / "Treating me like a person." / "Treating me like an adult." / "Treating me like an equal." / "Listening when you're approached by one of us." / "Trusting." / "Trusting me explicitly." / "Trusting me." / "Trusting my leadership of my team." / "Start trusting my judgments."*

Survey Question 3: In leading you, what do you want your boss to *stop* doing?

Here is the bad of the good news and bad news. We asked what the survey subjects wanted their leader to start doing, and also what they wanted their leader to *stop* doing. Figure 5.4 contains the word cloud that reflects the responses.

Go with impressions again. Decision-making references and the words "stop *being*" followed by myriad qualifiers seem to stand out. The emotions expressed in the sentiment pie (see Figure 5.5), as you could have guessed, have expanded in variety and intensity: anger, confusion, disgust, fear, worry, and surprise have all risen to reign emotionally where happiness used to rule. That's why they want you to stop it.

Read on to see, hear, and feel what our team members would like all of us to stop doing when we lead them.

FIGURE 5.4   What Do You Want Your Boss to Stop Doing?

FIGURE 5.5   Stop Doing—Basic Emotions Expressed

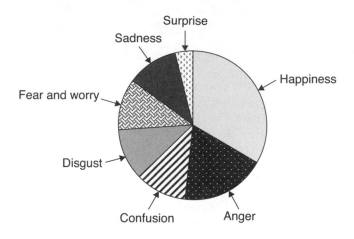

"Stop the spiteful, negative words and downgrading other people. Surely somewhere, someone has done something right." / "This isn't Miami Vice. We aren't good cop/bad cop. We are supposed to be a team!" / "Stop acting differently when in front of your bosses." / "Agreeing on a course of action with me and then reversing the decision." / "Allowing the squabbles between team members. You can make it stop." / "Asking me to do things without fully explaining why I am doing them. It's nice to understand the big picture." / "Asking what else you can do, and then not providing options or following through on what you say."

"Stop assuming your direction is totally understood." / "Assuming we know everything." / "Assuming bonus attainment is always a motivator. It's not." / "Assuming that we know you are pleased with the job that we are doing. You don't often say so." / "Avoiding team problems and hoping they will go away." / "Accommodating." / "Being quiet at times of crisis. At some point you have to say something" / "Being silent or in a bad mood when the workload increases." / "Believing that I can figure out most of the things on

74

my own." / "Comparing me with other people." / "Comparing our performance." / "Comparing me with other managers."

"Stop confronting people in public." / "Dictating the unjustifiable task." / "Discounting for lateness or laziness." / "Feigning interest or pretending to care." / "Just notice my missteps. Help me fix it." / "Telling us that you are there to help, if when we ask for help, the response is to be irritated with us." / "Looking in on me so much. Am I not trusted?" / "Stop drinking the Kool Aid. Stop making us do things without you fully understanding them." / "Enabling negativity within the team." / "Getting emotional/personal." / "Having someone else in the office during our one-on-one meetings." / "Having us do weekly reports that don't change and that no one reads anyways."

"Stop trying to control everything. You can't." / "He needs to stop letting things accumulate. Deal with problems when they occur." / "Stop hiding in your office."

"Stop holding back information that would help me improve." / "I am happy, satisfied, and can't think of anything that I would ask you to stop." [Authors' note: This response, or a version of, "There is nothing I want you to stop" came through 215 times.] / "I don't want my boss to stop doing anything. The support she supplies makes the business go around." / "Since I have no confirmation that you know what I do on a daily basis, I am concerned that you are making too many assumptions about the work I do." / "Stop rubbing in everyone's face that you are superior." / "Listen and stop rushing through every idea I bring up." / "Stop being so negative when we do hear from you, and let us know some good things as well." / "Stop excluding me as much as you do." / "I would like you to not speak for me in meetings."

"Stop trying to do everything yourself and include me on more tasks. I can lighten your load." / "Move away from doing so much 'fire fighting' and 'micromanaging.'" / "Stop ignoring my concerns." / "Ignoring my e-mails." / "Ignoring issues that need escalation." /

"Ignoring the team's concerns and suggestions." / "I'm more than twice your age—don't be condescending and treat me like a child." / "Jumping in too quickly." / "Leading by fear." / "Letting personal grievances affect our working environment." / "Making decisions based on state of mood for the day." / "Making decisions based on emotion rather than the bottom line." / "Making decisions prior to researching or discussing them." / "Making me feel intimidated." / "Making me feel rushed when I speak to you."

"Stop making pointless motivational presentations." / "Making promises that never get kept." / "Micromanaging" / "Micromanagement does not work. Show me what needs to be done, and then let me do it." / "Cancelling one-on-one sessions." / "Telling me to handle it, and then responding negatively to the way it has been handled." / "Forgetting what you promised." / "Overanalyzing, overreacting, overdelegating, overexplaining" / "Personal biases that hinder open and fair communication within the team." / "Giving vague answers when asked a specific question." / "Quit sending threats through e-mail." / "Redundancy in giving out orders." / "Relating the importance of the work only to the revenue it generates. Not everything can be a million-dollar project."

"Stop repeating the same discourse that the company tells you to repeat without evaluating our situations." / "Reprimanding in public and shouting on the floor." / "Saying no without listening." / "Saying what you think you need to say to make me feel good." / "Saying yes and not meaning it!" / "Sending me e-mails when we are just a few meters from each other." / "Sending us e-mails threatening disciplinary actions. Just do the disciplinary action if you need to." / "Promising good things to your people but not keeping your promises."

"Stop shouting or raising your voice to me." / "Showing preferences for one or two members of the team." / "Shrugging off feelings or emotions. They matter!" / "Sit with me during our one to ones and not behind your desk." / "Controlling to the point that I don't feel trusted." / "Correcting us in front of our subordinates." / "Sounding 'hurried' in our conversations." / "Stop acting like you can fire me at any time." / "Stop asking what I need from you. Let me do my work." / "Stop assuming I know everything. Sometimes I need help." / "Stop assuming that I know all processes that come with the post." / "Stop assuming that money is the only motivator." / "Stop assuming that you know every aspect of what I do each day."

"Stop being inconsistent, indecisive, indifferent, moody, negative, passive, sarcastic, self-centered, political, stubborn, perfectionist, insensitive, vague, invisible, disregarding, doubting, favoring, floating, forgetting, interrogating, interrupting." / "Communicating through e-mail only." / "Comparing me with other people." / "Micromanaging." / "Multitasking during our one on ones." / "Stop pointing fingers, preaching, pushing, pretending, shouting, showing, and talking down." / "Thinking I know it. I want to be encouraged sometimes." / "Thinking I'm a mind reader. I'm not." / "Waiting until the last minute to let us know if we are doing something wrong." / "Taking it personal." / "Commanding without knowledge of what to do." / "Focusing on the negative things, and giving more credit for the good ones." / "Walking away in the middle of an important conversation." / "Stop wanting to be always in control."

We asked for it, and we got it. What we just went through in what we should stop doing is essentially how we come across when we're ineffective in our leadership attempts. This is how we come across when we don't take the time to be present with those who matter to us. This is how we come across when we break the empathy connection.

Survey Question 4: In leading you, what do you want your boss to *continue* doing?

Here is the last of the personal change trifecta: what you should *continue* doing. Every one of you reading this is serious about

FIGURE 5.6   What Do You Want Your Boss to Continue Doing?

becoming a better leader. You are reading this work most likely because you are good at what you do, but you can always see room for improvement. Well, guess what? You already do lots of things right. Take a look at the word cloud above (Figure 5.6), and especially the sentiment pie chart (Figure 5.7), in reference to what you should continue to do. Powerful impressions, and of course, powerfully positive impressions. You already engage in many effective behaviors right now—these are the ones they want you to keep doing!

FIGURE 5.7   Continue Doing—Basic Emotions Expressed

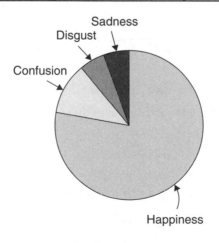

To give you the detail, here are the verbatim responses to the final question we asked around the globe—what your people want you to continue doing.

*"Continue being a servant leader who has a humble heart." /
"Accuracy and productivity in your work." / "Acknowledging positive work results by any staff member." / "Active participation and feedback." / "Allowing me the freedom to do my job." / "Allowing us to do our job without micromanagement." / "Allowing me to lead my team and only intervening when necessary." / "Allowing me to make decisions on my own. Thank you."*

"Allowing me to manage my own workload." / "Allowing us to do our job without constantly checking on us." / "Continue always being there." / "The pat on the back." / "Always supporting us, we appreciate it greatly." / "Always being there when needed." / "Appreciating my hard work." / "Asking for opinions and our input on processes."

*"Continue your attentiveness and dedication to the work." /
"Being human, not a machine." / "Being approachable and willing to help us as a team." / "Being approachable and treating us as 'individuals' instead of a group of employees." / "Being fair, flexible, friendly, honest, humble, professional, respectful, straightforward, supportive, helpful, thoughtful!" / "Being yourself." / "Being very helpful and thoughtful." / "Being a good example." / "Being a good listener." / "Being a good model." / "Being a nice, friendly yet a powerful leader who can have the whole team in control and performing."*

*"Continue caring about the team." / "Celebrating success." /
"Being friendly and generous." / "Respecting the fact that we have different approaches and working methods that are equally effective." / "Trusting me with what I do." / "Understanding my feelings and continuing to be sensitive to what I have been going through." / "Treating me like an equal and respecting my views." / "Treating*

us like a person that is very important to the company." / "Your offbeat sense of humor. We all need to laugh and keep ourselves sane." / "Empowering me." / "Explaining a lot, giving examples." / "Being flexible with requests." / "Providing feedback about what I'm doing right." / "Giving me the autonomy to manage my business." / "Giving kudos." / "Giving me a free rein to perform." / "Giving me suggestions to manage up." / "Trusting my judgment." / "Giving me the moral and morale support that I need." / "Giving positive feedback as it makes me feel valued, confident, and comfortable around you." / "Giving us our space." / "Giving visibility."

"Continue being a fair and strong leader." / "Showing support and respecting my views." / "Trusting my managing skills." / "Involving me in solving the problem." / "Being efficient, fair, flexible." / "Being someone who will listen without judging." / "Checking in with me." / "Being positive even when the situation is very difficult." / "Providing explanations to what you are looking for." / "Smiling." / "Talking; communication is the key to us all staying sane." / "Leading by example." / "Letting me run my business." / "Letting me run my department." / "Letting me do my job." / "Letting me do my style of work and not your style." / "Letting me do my work." / "Letting me know my metrics."

"Continue providing feedback and encouragement. You are outstanding!" / "Offering positive and negative feedback when appropriate." / "Your open door policy." / "Participation, partnership, passion, patience, persistence." / "Being approachable and always making time for me." / "Staying grounded no matter how much stress you are under." / "Professionalism." / "Respecting my knowledge, experience, skill." / "Setting attainable milestones." / "Correcting performance issues in private." / "Sharing best practices and practical experiences." / "Talking to me as an equal." / "Continue teaching me with patience."

The following is the integrated responses of many single-word responses that started with "continue being."

[Continue being] a people person, positive, strong, accessible, accountable, aggressive, appreciative, approachable, available, calm, caring, committed, creative, enthusiastic, flexible, focused, generous, happy, open minded, open to feedback, patient, pleasant, polite, positive, proactive, professional, punctual, there, true, trusting, understanding, updated.

Start, Stop, and Continue

Start, stop, and continue—the good, the bad, and the better. We'd like to round out this chapter with two more visuals and a few more verbatims. The word cloud (see Figure 5.1 at the beginning of this chapter) and emotion pie shown in Figure 5.8 are composites of all the stop-start-continue suggestions combined. What is your impression? Take a look for a moment. Then finish off the chapter with some very powerful and memorable insights from a few of our interview subjects, themselves experts on the subject of what to stop, start, and continue.

Jim Farley (group vice president, global marketing, sales and service, Ford Motor Company): Start caring, stop controlling,

FIGURE 5.8   Start-Stop-Continue—Composite

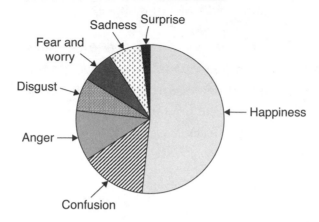

and continue being accountable for everlasting improvement. And, there's one other item I'd add: Find your higher calling. If you want to get more out of your team and you don't have resources (like we didn't at Ford for a while), you have to connect your staff to a higher calling. And I'm not talking about God; I'm talking about business—our work as managers or coaches. I think the opportunity or glue that holds it all together is the higher calling of our work. The higher calling of being a coach is the self-satisfaction that comes really after your career is done, knowing you've given the gift of excellence to others.

And I'll give you an example. When I first got here I asked the head of global engineering, "I want to know what makes these engineers tick. What makes these Ford engineers different from Toyota engineers?" And he said, "Jim, I think they should answer that question." So I spent two days roaming around our engineering labs in Dearborn. It seemed literally miles and miles. So I wandered into our safety lab, and I met one of the guys who was about 50-something years old, introduced myself, and he says,

"Oh, you're the new guy from Toyota." So I said, "Yep. Tell me what you're doing here."

"I'm saving lives," he says.

It turned out that this guy was a doctor who started his career as a practicing physician at the Philadelphia Children's Hospital, but then he lost his own daughter in an automobile accident. So he decided to leave his very profitable practice in Philly and join Ford. So I asked him, "Why did you join Ford?" He responded, "Because I knew I could save more lives, and I never want others to have to go through what I did when I lost my teenage child."

And then he said, "Let me show you what I'm doing," and he showed me a crash test dummy with a gelatin stomach. "The government doesn't require us to have a teenaged crash-test dummy to test. And Ford doesn't require me to put a gelatin stomach to simulate the undeveloped belly of a 12-year-old child. My daughter died of internal bleeding, and her lower intestines were dramatically different from those of adults. So for us to make cars and our belt systems safer, I knew I had to, as a doctor, duplicate the anatomy of a 12- or 13-year-old in a crash-test dummy. Because of that we have completely changed the way our body engineering is done."

So I said, "You're really coming into work each day thinking you're saving lives?"

"My greatest moment is when I'm driving home and I pass an accident on the road, and there is a parent and a child on the cell phone calling their loved one saying everything is okay. *That* is why I come to work at Ford. I know that when I'm retired, I'll feel like I've pushed and pushed the company to do the right thing," he said.

So I think whatever it is, whatever we do, if we don't have a higher calling like that man has, we won't be able to successfully cope with the no-normal world.

Chuck Sykes (president and CEO, Sykes Enterprises): Start innovating; stop creating self-imposed barriers with your ego. Stop making your decisions based on your past knowledge. Just as you said, there is no new normal. And continue learning—lifelong learning, learning to adapt.

Marshall Goldsmith (author, speaker, and coach): Start learning. Stop trying to be right all the time and continue with integrity.

Howard Morgan (author, coach, and managing director of the Leadership Research Institute): Stop being an employee. Stop being staff; start being a leader! Most can't let go of their need to know everything and be in control. Just as you mentioned in a parenting context, *start letting go*. Continue relying on your instinct and your gut to guide you in the right direction. When leaders make mistakes, it's when they ignore the voice in the back of their head saying, "It's a stupid idea, don't do it!" At an absolute minimum, listen to your inner voice and then make the decision.

At the start of this chapter we said communication, praise and recognition, performance review, and independence are the beginnings of the new rules of engagement. In the next section we'll help you get organized to make the most effective use of this powerful message.

GETTING READY

You've studied the game, the rules, and the playing field. You understand the team, the players, and what they want from you. It's now time to fully prepare for the challenges that lay ahead:

o **Untapped talent.** *Where* will you find it? Your core team members are waiting to be asked. Discretionary performance is theirs to give, and it's time to ask for it.
o **Anatomy of communication.** What happens between you and your team members in the moment is *what* activates additional capacity. Understand human communication in a business setting, understand yourself, and understand what matters.

CHAPTER 6

Untapped Talent: Targeting the Core of Your Team

What you focus on expands. Period. You heard it decades ago from the likes of Wayne Dyer, an internationally renowned author and speaker in the field of self-development, and you can hear the same message today from Oprah. What we focus on, think about, look at, listen to, and involve ourselves in will grow and expand within our lives. Think about it for a moment. If you spend your days listening to Rush Limbaugh, The O'Reilly Factor, and Sean Hannity, what will you tend to see more of? Socialist conspiracies? Liberal vendettas? The crumbling of the very fabric of American society and values? What if you spend those same waking hours connected to Bill Maher, Arianna Huffington, and CNN? What would you then tend to believe and espouse? The crying need for the wealthy to pay their fair share? Ruthless bankers and business executives taking unfair advantage? The innate, almost laughable ignorance of the conservative viewpoint? What we focus on expands. The good, the bad, and the ugly.

In Section One, "A New Era," we positioned the necessity of capacity without headcount. You need more output, but you're not likely to get more help. We isolated the decay of the human connection with the empathy crash of 2000 and what it's going to take to lead in the next decade when we won't know enough to be experts anymore. In Section Two, "Just Ask Me," we consolidated thousands of responses from people just like you and your teammates. We gave global voice to what our people want us to know and do. We know enough now. We have the context. Now it's time to prepare ourselves as leaders. Here in Section Three, "Getting Ready," we turn your focus to where you can have the biggest impact, the highest return—on the *core* of your team. We also give you a powerful basic anatomy of interactions, a model for understanding and replicating success in the moment with your people. Let's start with a different focal point for leading in a no-normal world.

Leading at the Top of the Curve

We're betting that most of you have heard of the tenet of a "normal distribution curve." It has to do with probability theory and states that in most situations with a population of any real size, we can pretty much count on results being distributed across a bell-shaped curve. For just about anything in life—*including leadership*—normal distribution theory states that we can anticipate 15 percent at one extreme, 15 percent at the other end, and 70 percent falling somewhere within two groups in the middle. This tells us that in our groups, our *teams*, we'll have a small subgroup of performers at one extreme, another small group at the opposite end, and a very large group turning in performance that falls somewhere right in the middle. Let's take this rule of thumb and apply it, with some revision, to our advantage.

It stands to reason that if 70 percent of our people fall into a particular performance grouping, then that's probably where we'd spend 70 percent of our time and energy. Right? Wrong. When we've asked thousands of leaders in our workshops where they spend the majority of their emotional energy and time, their answers invariably reflect a theme of: *"I spend way too much of my time with one or two 'problem children' situations that just won't go away!"* The "victims" who always have an answer for why their work isn't done. The naysayer who pokes holes in any proposed solution. The team member you avoid contact with because it's easier to just do it yourself. The person who gives everyone else that tight feeling just seeing his or her vehicle in the parking lot in the morning. This is one end of the normative distribution curve. It's a very small group of people, but the problem is that they take up the majority of your time and energy. Whenever we hear a description of this type of problem child situation from a participant, we always then ask the entire audience: "How many of you have a situation like this going on right now?" Most hands go up. We follow up with "How many of your situations have been going on for at least a year?" Most hands *stay* up, maybe even sheepishly inch up a little higher.

That's one extreme of our collective workforce, but it's not the classic 15 percent of the curve. It's much less. We mentioned that the incidence of totally negative responses to our survey questions was less than 7 percent. Only *6.8 percent* of the more than 6,000 responses came from a problem child perspective. Perhaps the leadership curve carries a different shape. Let's look at the other extreme of our collective workforce. Ever hear the term "hi-po"? A high-potential employee is usually defined as an individual who has been identified as having what it takes to move up into more senior roles and responsibilities. Most organizations formally acknowledge these folks as having made the list and then establish a path for their upward mobility that includes quite a few stops along the way. The high-potential receives a lot of attention, and perhaps for good reason. Consider first, though, how big of a group is it? How important is this group of people? In the *Harvard Business Review* or the Society for Human Resource

Management, the consensus seems to be that the high-potential employee represents only 2 to 3 percent of a workforce. On top of that, on any given day, up to one-third of them are already actively seeking employment elsewhere. This extreme of the leadership bell curve also takes on a different slope.

As leaders we've got 1 or 2 percent of our people at one extreme looking out into their future from the heights of high potential. At the other end of our collective curve, we've got another 6 or 7 percent of our team members camped in the depths of the problem zone. Unfortunately, this 7 to 9 percent of our workforce seems to siphon off significant amounts of our energy. We're leading at the ends of the curve, and a no-normal world won't allow that. Shift your focus to the *top of the curve*. In practice, over 90 percent of our capacity is maintained by very little of our attention. What might we achieve by taking on a new leadership focus? Over 90 percent of our capacity is waiting on us—waiting to be asked, waiting to engage. The core of your team is waiting for *you*. Stay with us now to learn how to identify who makes up the core of your team. We'll show you how to avoid or eliminate the problem child trap (you can even delegate problem children to human resources). Discover the high-potential paradox, and maybe leave that challenge to the organizational development department. Shift *your* focal point. The core of your team is where you can create additional capacity without more headcount. Learn to lead at the top of the curve!

Solve the Problem: Free Up the Capacity

Let's start with the low end of the curve where, ironically, we can free up maximum capacity. It may seem counterintuitive, but by addressing the area where performance is lowest, we free up valuable resources where the return is highest—ourselves. Most leaders we work with have a problem scenario they would like to take care of, many that have gone on for not just months but years. At some point, a wait-and-see-strategy becomes simple avoidance. When it comes to confirmed performance problems, there is an inverse relationship between pace and pain; the quicker we are at addressing an issue, the sooner we're freed up, and pain disappears. The two of us have trained and spoken in front of many thousands of frontline managers, and we have never heard a leader say, "I fired that person way too quickly. I should have let it go on much longer." Never. Ever. Also having five daughters between us, we have also never heard a young woman say, "I broke up with him way too soon." Allow us to give you the tools you can use to face problems and solve them; how to identify truly regressive situations, how to then address them by leveraging what you give versus what they want, and finally how to balance consequences and follow a healthy hierarchy of reinforcement.

So how do you identify the problem child scenario? How do you know when something should move from coaching to discipline? A couple of case studies can help illustrate the process.

Case 1: Roberto worked in sales. In a very competitive environment, quality leads were at a premium. One of several sales reps, Roberto carried a large book of business and enjoyed a certain amount of political capital because of his success. He has been anxious about a downturn in sales over the last year and has begun crossing the line to keep his sales and commission structure at the level he feels he deserves. Roberto has taken to coming in after hours to pick up all the hard-copy inquiries from the fax when no one else is there (they would normally be divided up equally the next day). He's even gone so far as to manipulate CRM inquiry records from the website to backdate his "ownership" of new leads.

Case 2: Beth was an administrative assistant who reported to Bob, the account director. John was a newly hired account executive who also reported to Bob. Beth's job is to support the sales and project management efforts of both Bob and John. Over a 12-month period Beth doted on Bob, but found every reason under the sun to not be available for John's work, or she made sure the output was inconsistent, late, or unacceptable. John, being younger and new to the organization, isn't sure how to address the problem with Beth. He tried reasoning and being nicer and finally ended up using work-arounds just to avoid the tension of dealing with Beth.

Let's get the easy one out of the way first. If it involves an ethics violation, fire the individual. Follow whatever progressive discipline guidelines your organization has to remove the person (not just a transfer). Roberto in case 1 is guilty of several breaches of ethics. If you know about them, you can count on *everyone* knowing about them. Even if he is protected by a senior manager, follow your company's procedures and begin the process for termination. Demand courage from your human resources department. It's akin to removing a Band-Aid; the faster you pull it off, the less it hurts.

The best method we know of to identify when to move from coaching to discipline involves the rule of three. Have you ever heard of *the rule of three?* If you look, you'll see triads everywhere: musical chords, comedy, and literature, the holy trinity. In fact, the entire organizational structure of the U.S. Marine Corps is based on threes (Google it!). What does this have to do with effective leadership? We can't tell you how many times participants asked, "How will I know when to get involved in a situation?" "How do I know when someone has gained some level of mastery?" "How do I know if someone has an attitude problem or is just having a bad day?" For all these we invoke the rule of three—the lowest number of data points it takes to either establish or discard a pattern. In making decisions regarding the people who matter to you, consider the following:

1. **If you know of three examples of nonperformance,** there is a performance problem. Get involved.
2. **When you observe three demonstrations of mastery,** they get it. What's your exit strategy with them? It's time to delegate!
3. **After three incidents of nonperformance coupled with anger, bitterness, or an attitude problem,** it is a call to action to you. Find out why things are the way they are, and be ready to move from coaching to discipline.

As we move on to addressing the situation you've now acknowledged is a problem, we'd like to plant this thought: discipline, not punishment and resolution, not revenge. The trap many of us fall into lies in waiting too long and letting tension build too high before we address an obvious problem. At that point issues come to the surface with a heavy emotional load and usually don't end well. If you are following the pace/pain formula, you've addressed it *now* and haven't let months (or years) of bad blood build up. Unlike societal discussions on the purpose of imprisoning convicted offenders, this involves neither punishment nor rehabilitation. The purpose is resolution and completion for *you*. The objective is to remove the situation from your radar, nothing more, nothing less. If performance improves, great. It's off your list. There's a classic four-quadrant decision-making model that combines your priority with employees' performance. It is the quadrant where high priority and low performance meet that we are concerned with here. The strategy is to keep the problem child quadrant empty so you can focus your efforts on the core. Now, some techniques for resolution.

We all hear a lot about motivation, but for most it remains a mystery. We can clear that up. Think about case 2, with Beth. There is no ethics violation in play, but there is a problem; John is not being supported in his work (with customers, we might add). When it comes to problem scenarios like the one with Beth, keep in mind that it's *you* who is motivated. You are the one who is motivated to see something different happen. Beth is most likely happy with business as usual. She doesn't want to help John. Motivation is intrinsic. It's inside of us. It's very difficult to create motivation in someone else, but you can create movement in the right direction. Movement comes from the application of consequences and using them to reinforce the movement you desire (movement in your direction). As you consider how to create movement in one of your people, first study the hierarchy of consequences. Consequences revolve around what you give and what employees want:

1. **Give/what they want.** Known as positive reinforcement or reward, this involves giving employees what they want when you see the movement you desire.
2. **Don't give/what they want.** Known as extinction or withholding, this involves not providing what they want until you see movement in the right direction. Putting behaviors on extinction essentially means ignoring or not reacting to another's attempts to get your attention.
3. **Don't give/what they don't want.** Known simply as rescue, taking away a negative consequence, or pulling the proverbial thorn from the lion's paw, can be a very powerful catalyst toward movement.
4. **Give/what they don't want.** This is known as negative reinforcement or punishment. Keep in mind that this inhibits movement. Granted, it can be very effective at stopping movement away from your goal, but it generally won't create movement *toward* what you do want. This is a last resort. This is the official progressive discipline process. This often helps someone succeed elsewhere. This is where HR courage enters the picture.

The last suggestion in the way of guidance we'd like to give you here lies in understanding what moves us, the very nature

94

of consequences. If you are applying consequences, there are no cookie-cutter answers. If anyone tells you there are easy steps to handling difficult people, don't believe it. Consequences are as individualized as it gets, but there are parameters. If you want to create movement, you need consequences that are personal, immediate, and certain. This applies to the rewards you give as well. If the consequences are organizational in nature, if they are delayed, or if there is uncertainty as to whether you really mean it (and will back up your promises), you won't create any real-time movement. Consequences that create movement are personal; they have an impact on that one individual. Consequences that create movement are immediate; they take effect now, not next quarter or next year. Consequences that create movement are certain; people believe you (even better, they've seen proof).

If you follow this path of maximum pace/minimum pain, heeding the rule of three, aiming for resolution, not revenge, movement, not motivation, and understanding and applying the right consequences, your "problem quadrant" will stay empty and you can take a big first step toward freeing yourself to lead at the top of the curve. Peter Drucker, the father of management, is famous for his observation that, "We spend a lot of time teaching leaders what to do. We don't spend enough time teaching leaders what to stop doing." Stop spending 90 percent of your time and energy trying to engage 6.8 percent of your people. Free yourself to engage the core of your team.

The Heights of High Potential

Potential is what is possible—what we are capable of but have not yet realized. All organizations strive to identify their high-potential employees. Most organizations today even inform those who made the list, either formally or informally. Initially, the purpose of identifying high-potential talent was that of helping organizations maintain their leadership pipelines, their steady flow of tomorrow's leaders—identifying and developing those with the drive, spirit, smarts, and emotional intelligence to excel in more senior positions. Knowing who could cut it at the next level was the driver behind the efforts of identifying those with high potential. What does this have to do with you?

Each of us works under unique circumstances, yet no-normal is universal. We've said that the hi-po population makes up at most 2 to 3 percent of the average organization. In some cases in some professions, it's less than 1 percent. We said that up to a third of the hi-po population is already seeking active employment elsewhere. In the best of times only 8 to 9 percent of your team members even have a chance to make the list of 2 percent. How much of your mental shelf space are you giving to this future-focused quadrant? How much should you be giving to it?

Succession planning is important. Take into consideration two critical factors, though, in deciding how much of your focus gets dedicated to it; hi-pos require different ingredients for a different type of almost conditional engagement, and your time and attention is a zero-sum resource. Hi-pos are accustomed to organizations providing greater amounts of visibility, access, status, special assignments, and next-level development. They also ask for significant career advancement and authority as prerequisites to engagement. We ask you: can you afford it? Can you afford large amounts of your emotional energy to be dedicated to this effort, or should that wait? Should that resource commitment be moved from interpersonal overhead, a fixed expense, to a transactional variable expense that you routinely assess but not necessarily invest in? The effort you save can be dedicated to the core of your team. For now, leave the hi-po debate to those in organizational development. A higher potential payout can be achieved with the core members of your team. They are waiting. They don't require as much. The return can be massive.

Targeting the Core of Your Team

We've given you ideas for perhaps what to stop doing to allow yourself the freedom to focus on the top of the curve. Now for the final ingredient—finding the core of your team. We conducted a powerful roundtable with a pair of practitioners supremely qualified to help us get to know the core of the team. We gave them our questions concerning understanding and identifying the core of a team, and turned them loose. We'd like to begin with a quote from another of our favorite practitioners.

Davis L. Holloway is an experienced master leadership trainer, having trained and coached thousands of practicing managers. His background is unique in that his decades in human resources and training and development span both public and private enterprises. Over five years with Southwest Airlines followed a full career as an officer in the U.S. Air Force. He sums up his perspective on core team members to get us started:

> When I think of who my core team members are, I listen to my inner voice. It describes consistently reliable output, not episodic performance. Those who exhibit and demonstrate a positive and supportive attitude, whatever the context, embody the core of my team. At Southwest this was actually a performance review rated item—"Southwest Spirit." Those who appear actively engaged in contributing—they are the core of my team. Members who exemplify and inspire others. They are responsible for themselves, and they have a positive effect on other team members; that's the core of my team. The core of my team is made up of those who populate my mental list of employees that I am proud of.
>
> Any team member can be a core member. They can exhibit every level of readiness for different objectives and still be a core team member. And I'll tell you what. Give me a workforce of even 50 to 60 percent of employees who fit the above, and I will be able to move mountains.

Read on for more practitioner-based guidance on understanding, identifying, and engaging the core of your team. The practitioners are:

Timothy Srock, vice president of human resources at McLaren Regional Medical Center in Flint, Michigan. Prior to his position within McLaren, he led human resources departments at St. John Health System, Compuware Corporation, and R.L. Polk.

Troy Van Hauen, director of human resources for The Maschhoffs in southwestern Illinois. The Maschhoffs manages one of the largest family-owned pork production networks in the United States, producing more than 2 million pigs annually.

Tim Srock: From my perspective it's complexity that makes it tough on the leader, and it makes an engaged core a nonnegotiable. The average manager needs to know an awful lot today: financials, operations, psychology of people, laws and regulations, and even the complexity of it on the people side. The books talk about baby boomers and gen X, the complexity of what each person brings to the job and what each one needs from us is far higher than it ever was. Then bring in the issue of speed; everything is end of day/end of week. The shortcutting that exists is interfering with the long-term economic stability of our organizations. Speed and complexity are making it much more difficult to lead effectively than just a few of years ago.

Troy Van Hauen: And the main difference between today and five years ago is the economy—the jobs that have been lost, the wealth that has been lost. Because of that, I think there's a very large disenfranchised talent pool out there of people who are very capable and talented professionals, who want to work and please, are positive and motivated, but find no jobs for them, or remain highly vulnerable in the one they have. When you strip it down, uncertainty hurts everybody, and there is a greater need now more than ever to provide a tangible result from human capital investments. It's a priority. We've got two wars going on, and the world is unstable. And the wars in some sense are about oil. There isn't a business I've worked for in the last 20 years where energy didn't have a major impact. Even on a personal level, everyone knows someone who's deployed. When it knocks our people off their game, it makes it tough on their leaders too. Understanding and engaging that core of the team is essential today. Just having the job isn't enough on its own. It's time to target them.

Tim Srock: And, I think from a frontline manager's perspective, identifying a team's core is about establishing the expectations first and then applying them to the people you have in place. People come and go, but the standard and consistency is the key to a team's core. Some of the managers I've worked with have done that. One in particular is Anita Sparks. She was a nurse manager we hired, and her work unit was one of those units where, once people were hired into the organization, they lined up to transfer to her department. It wasn't that she was the smartest manager in the world or anything like that, but she established expectations over a long period of time and was consistent in leading to those expectations. There was no surprise day in and day out in what was expected of you. It's simple to say, but it's very complex to do. It takes time, and the employees have to trust and believe in what the managers are doing, follow them and support them, even when the manager isn't there.

Troy Van Hauen: I love it. Let's add to your theme of expectations. It's an integrated philosophy we've modified into our talent management, where you have critical roles and critical talents.

Here's the premise and the philosophy: clearly, everyone is created equal. There's no question about that. Clearly, what evidence also suggests is that not every role is created equal. In other words, not every role drives the same value. This is part of our expectations setting. You identify those critical roles that really drive heavy value. That's the first thing you do. Then you start to identify in your core team who really drives the value, and also what the secondary roles are that protect that wealth. Let's put it in pig terms. One of our chief drivers of value is, how many pigs that sow has, and how many she keeps alive. We have an expectation around "day-one care," and the person responsible for that high-value role is a great candidate for the core of the team. To be effective as leaders, we need to understand the roles we fill, as well as the people in them.

Tim Srock: Once we have expectations set, then the way I've worked to identify the individuals over the years is threefold. First, I look at the product of their work. Core members produce, and you can always tell core team players because their output is measurable. Their output may go up or down, but it's always measurable. If you have a team member whose work is not measurable, you're likely headed for a problem. It's not always numbers. It might be the quality of people they hire, the turnaround on phone calls, requests to them, or just the nature of the feedback you get from others. But it is measurable. The second key variable is what I've always known as disproportionate influence. The people who are the core of the team are the people who others go to. Even though their job title or their pay grade might not reflect it, people come to them because they are strong at what they do, and they're respected. For me those are the first two variables that define the core of the team: who is creating measurable output and what is their relationship with and impact upon their teammates. In all my years working I'd say only 1 or 2 percent of the terminations

I've been a part of were related to an inability to perform. They were invariably based on impact on others. I too follow your rule of three, and I've often used it to describe the problem child aberrations: "once is luck, twice is skill, and three times is a pattern." Anyone can make a mistake once; after it happens again, they are starting to get good at it, and at three times it's a pattern engrained into their performance. The rule of three works at both ends of the curve.

The last cue for me is that the members of the core of a team want to learn. By nature, engaged human beings are always looking to do more, learn more, and expand their boundaries. I had a project where it was my responsibility for the entire corporation to implement an applicant and requisitions tracking system. I wanted the core team to help me implement this. What I did *not* do was go out and ask the superstars or the high-potentials. I did my homework, talked to a variety of people, and asked the right questions to determine who would not only have the technical skill to do it but would have the ability to think systemically and not just how their subsidiary does things. By pulling together this core group of people, we rolled out, in relatively short order for a complex organization, a very good system. They embraced the new—the rush of readiness you get when you grow with the job.

Troy Van Hauen: That's a good thing too, because the jobs, the roles themselves are evolving. What might be a high-value role today, an "A" role, in a year and a half becomes a "B" role. The role can move from wealth-generating to wealth-protecting. We need both direct-to-value and support-to-value roles, but they can change sometimes without our even realizing it. You know your core team members by how they react to the change in their roles. Just as you say, core team members embrace the rush, the evolution. I like the way this conversation is evolving. You know core team members by their output, the measurability of their performance, their impact on others, and their agility or adaptability in responding to how we're all evolving in this no-normal world.

If you ask me, you can also identify the core member in what they want from you. Don and Bill, your research is right on. They want communication, guidance, praise; and the independence isn't just autonomy, it's the authority to try. Don't punish me when I make mistakes. What, research says most of us make small mistakes 30 to 35 percent of the time? Core team members cry for the room to make those mistakes safely. What the core team member gets out of it is horizontal and vertical development. They get to evolve. They gain scalability in themselves. I recently met someone I worked for years ago. She wasn't doing well professionally, and we spent quite some time together in a coaching conversation. When we were done, she said, "Troy, you're not at all as I remember you. You were a wild man back then, but today you've had a huge impact on my life." I thanked her and said we knew each other long ago, and that right now I see myself as Troy-version 15. What version are you today? She stared at me with a blank face and said, "I don't know." As you said, Tim, core team members strive to grow and evolve, the same way their world is evolving around them.

Powerful observations from two very astute and very experienced leaders. Our conversations with Tim and Troy have given us usable, operational parameters for identifying the core of our teams:

○ **Output:** Core members get things done.
○ **Measurability:** It may rise and fall, but their performance is always trackable.

- ○ **Interpersonal impact:** The effect they have on their teammates and the influence potential they possess is disproportionate to their title.
- ○ **Adaptability:** They possess the resilience to evolve along with their role.

This is what stands out at the top of the curve—the core of our team. If you want to create capacity without headcount, *stop* spending your mental shelf space and emotional energy at the ends of the bell curve. *Start* leading at the top of the curve, the core of the team, and *continue* embracing the evolution of your role.

CHAPTER 7

Anatomy of Communication: Preparing to Lead in the Moment

N ow you know *where* you need to focus your efforts. You've targeted the core team members, and what happens between you and them in the moment is *what* will activate additional capacity. You are the catalyst, not some new performance management system, not another realignment of compensation systems, not another spirited articulation of organization vision. Your interactions in the moment are what turn on added effort or turn it off. Our workshop participants invariably tell us that 90 percent of their leadership interactions with their team members aren't planned, they aren't scheduled. They are spontaneous interactions, impromptu messages exchanged in the moment. We think you can best prepare yourself to be more effective in the moment by making sure you fully understand the dynamics of human interaction by getting to know a simple anatomy of communication.

Anatomy is the science or study of structure. Believe it or not, leadership interactions in a no-normal world are not as crazy as they seem. Rules still apply. Structure can be discerned in your daily communication with others. With a little preparation you *can* make sense of all the noise. To do that, we've invited in Mr. C. D. Morgan to join us for this chapter. "Hoop" Morgan, as he's known, is the founder and chairman of the Forté Institute in Wilmington, North Carolina. Communication is his business, his passion, and his life. Along with Hoop, we're going to reorganize your thinking around human interaction, especially human communication in this age of abbreviation and interruption.

Let's establish a premise right off the bat. In high-stress environments, how we approach challenges typically predicts the outcome. Our approach governs where we end up, and the mind is the fastest way to travel. Consider the following:

o What we think, especially our thoughts about ourselves, can intensify the stress we experience from other sources.
o These emotions seem to be even worse when we begin something we've never tried before.
o The law of cause and effect operates in our lives, whether we understand it or not and whether we believe it or not.
o What we believe, or whatever dominates our thinking, will result in interpersonal experiences that reflect those thought patterns.
o It's not enough just to think positively. We have to recognize old ineffective patterns and then have the awareness not to give them new life.
o We are what we repeatedly think and do. Excellence, then, is not an act, but rather a habit.
o Being engulfed by a situation over which you seem to lack control can create a strong sense of helplessness. But just as feelings of pessimism and despair can be learned, so can optimism.
o The process and structure coming up involves perhaps changing deeply ingrained habits of thought. The long-term results

can be dramatic, but remember that improvement and growth are always gradual.

o Our goal here is to let you see your leadership interactions through an accurate, yet solution-based structure, while at the same time, hopefully reframing your habits of thought about communication in general and business communication in particular.

Development of Thought

The best place for us to start is with a little backstory. Personal profiling as we know it today had its genesis in the work of Jung, Marston, Jacobi, Briggs, and a few others. These early attempts to understand personality really took off after World War II. We can trace the growth and development of thought around human communication as we can with most anything else today—follow the money. Back in the late 1940s the National Institute of Health decided to begin profiling military personnel in a big way. The original psychometric questionnaires were designed to measure psychological preferences and patterns in how we perceive and interact with the world. The variables early on, and even to this day, are essentially measuring degrees of assertiveness and responsiveness.

How assertive are you, and how responsive are you when you interact with others? The consensus seems to be that about 70 percent of who we are in this fashion is nurture and 30 percent nature. In other words, 70 percent of who we are is made up of environmentally conditioned traits (how our life has formed us), and only 30 percent is made up of the genetically inherited traits beyond our control. This is good news because it suggests that we can recondition ourselves. Interestingly enough, most profiling— personality, communication, or behavioral—measures only the primarily inherited traits, the 30 percent that in most of us is set by the age of 10.

Also across the majority of profiling tools and approaches are varying degrees of what's called *validity* and *reliability*. In reference to a profiling questionnaire, statistical validity and reliability refer to two very important measures: Does the instrument in fact measure what it says it measures, and does the instrument in fact do so at an acceptable level of consistency? Some models and instruments make claims that they can't back up. Some have enjoyed great commercial success without classical validation; they may be popular, but they are not reliable. What we are going to reveal for you now is a communication style model that is the standard of validity and reliability. It measures more than just assertiveness and responsiveness, and reflects your tendencies formed by both nature and nurture and does so with 40 years of commercial success behind it as well. It is the Forté Interpersonal Communication System. Forté refers to one's strength or most highly developed characteristic or competency. What are *your* communication strengths? Read on.

Interpersonal Communication: Organized for You

While people are generally aware that they have communication strengths that govern their everyday behavior or communication style, they are often not aware that these communication styles are well defined, even obvious, and that they produce specific and unique profile patterns. An individual's communication style can be determined, shared, and enhanced (you *can* change it). In most profiles, a primary communication style strength, one of four, will be evident. Depending upon the intensity, this single strength will control your attitude, action, and responses up to 60 percent of the time.

The following information will assist you in understanding the characteristics of the four primary strengths. Keep in mind that these strengths reflect how you think, understand, relate, and come across to others; there is tremendous value in knowing your communication style characteristics and the characteristics of others.

1. **Dominance/Nondominance—The Decision Strength** *(from dominant to nondominant or controlling to cooperative).* The dominant or controlling person is results-oriented and primarily concerned with getting things done. Dominant people are hard-driving and to the point, and they dislike indecisiveness. They appear outwardly secure, and are innovative, venturesome, ingenious, big-picture–oriented, and sometimes abrasive. They are troubleshooters, decisive, and risk takers.

   The nondominant or cooperative person is characterized by a nonthreatening way of working with others. This person is not forcefully demanding. A nondominant person will seldom impose upon others, is mild-mannered, composed, and often modest. They are still decision makers; they just appreciate input from others before making their decisions. They genuinely prefer your input.

2. **Extroversion/Ambiversion/Introversion—The People Strength** *(from extroverted to introverted or outgoing to reserved).* The extrovert or outgoing person is people-oriented. Extroverts are friendly, pleasant, persuasive, emphatic, enthusiastic, talkative, stimulating, motivating, and optimistic. They are good mixers and good coordinators. The extrovert likes to be with and influence people. They are verbal. They are drawn to others.

   Ambiverts are the center point of the dimension of extroversion and introversion. They can move easily between seeking to

109

be with others to just being by themselves to think things over or to communicate one on one.

Introverted or reserved people are selective in whom they place their trust; they take greater care in protecting their private life and prefer not to speak without weighing the potential consequences. They are creative and have an individualistic side that can manifest itself in a vivid imagination and the ability to think things through to a conclusion. They tend to be contemplative, they enjoy quiet, and they do not need others around for self-fulfilling activities.

3. **Patience/Impatience—The Pace Strength** *(from patient to impatient or paced to urgent):* The patient or paced individual is relaxed, easygoing, steady, amiable, warm, dependent, sincere, likable, and a good listener. The paced person likes peace and harmony, likes to be cooperative, likes to save time, and likes time to adjust to changes. Their first answer is typically not their best answer. This has nothing to do with intelligence; they simply prefer some time to think things over before answering.

The impatient or urgent person is action-oriented and does not tolerate delays for extended periods of time. This person often has to do things twice for lack of adequate planning. Impatient people have a strong sense of urgency, both for themselves and for those around them. It is important for these individuals to keep busy and have others respond quickly to them. They learn quickly and prefer variety as opposed to a single area of concentration. Their sense of urgency often drives them to seek out new, exciting situations that offer them a change of pace.

4. **Conformity/Nonconformity—The Systems Strength** *(from conformist to nonconformist or systematic to independent):* The conformist or systematic person, depending upon environment and experience, will be careful, accurate, precise, thorough,

skillful, dependable, meticulous, conservative, prudent, anxiety-prone, worried, sensitive to criticism, and a perfectionist. Liking details and systems, this person prefers to work systematically, wants outcomes to be correct, and wants to be fair.

The nonconformist or independent person is characterized by a generalist orientation to life. This person often shows a rather independent attitude, with a tendency to avoid or delegate detail work. These individuals usually are uninhibited and candid, and they relate well to activities that take them out of ordinary or prescribed situations. These individuals want freedom and minimal controls, both in work and personal relationships. They can be resistant to controls and will tend to rationalize.

How we make decisions, our need for people, our sense of urgency, and our attention to detail—these are the variables that make up the anatomy of communication. Decisions. People. Pace. Detail. Are you controlling or cooperative? Extroverted or introverted? Patient or impatient? Conforming or independent? Wait until later in the chapter. We give you the opportunity to find out. For now, see Figure 7.1 for the profile of one of the authors (Don) and his primary pattern.

In Don's profile there are four columns representing the communication strengths of dominance (dom), extroversion (ext), patience (pat), and conformity (con). There is a scale of 0 to 36 above the center line and another of 0 to 36 below the center line. Don's profile is 24 above in dominance, 22 above in extroversion, 9 below the center line in urgency, and 23 below the center line in nonconformity. There is much, much more information available in the report, but let's cover some of the basics of what we know from Don's profile as a dominant, extroverted, impatient, nonconformist:

FIGURE 7.1   Don's Forté Primary Profile

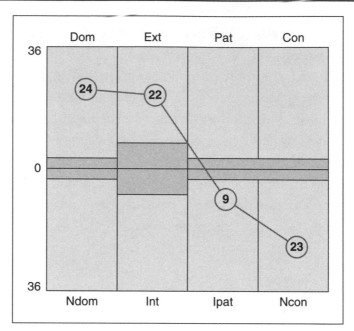

○ Don is personable and can use either a persuasive style or direct commands when communicating with others. He is results- and big-picture oriented. Typically he is aggressive, very competitive, and independent. He is a nonconformist and wants to find better ways to do things in a way that vary from tradition or rules. He makes quick decisions and takes risks.

○ Characteristic of intense-dominance individuals is their hard-driving, to-the-point nature. They are big-picture–oriented, risk takers, and outwardly secure. Often Don is not aware of how strongly he comes across to other people. His primary concern is getting things done, and he can be pleasant and generous as long as he is getting results. Don prefers to give orders rather than take them and is most productive when he is on his own and not under close supervision. Typical of intense dominance is the desire to solve complex problems and respond to a challenge. His leadership style is that of an authoritative manager who performs his leadership role by direct command. He is inner-directed with a lot of self-confidence in his ability to get things done. He tends to take on more work and is slow to delegate authority. Sensitive areas include too many external controls or trivial interferences. If he feels that he is being forced into a corner, he will come across as a steamroller or dictator to gain control of a situation.

o People with the same characteristics as Don assume authority readily and are powerful decision makers. They will respect authority or organizations when they are results-oriented. They tend to feel that they can accomplish anything. They like to explore areas removed from tradition and the system and tend to relate to freedom and flexibility. They commonly create new customs and rules. They take charge in a very convincing way. They are fairly friendly and self-confident with individuals. They tend to be persuasive and amiable with others until resistance occurs; then they are very direct. The emphasis is on fast, fluent, to-the-point communications. They not only want results, but they want them right now. The strength pairing of dominance and impatience causes them to be self-starters, very competitive, and ambitious.

You can tell a lot about someone just having an "anatomy" to go on. Dominance, extroversion, patience (pace), and conformity. What about *your* profile? How do *you* prefer to make decisions? What is your need for interacting with others? Your sense of urgency and systems orientation? Perhaps a little more background can strengthen our case even further. How do we know that assertiveness and responsiveness aren't all that matters in *business* communication? What told us that pace and conformity mattered just as much? How do we know that these four variables are the ones that matter? This model, while classically validated, was developed commercially rather than clinically. Countless approaches to communication were developed in a clinical context and then later applied to a business setting. This anatomy was first conceived in response to a client request for help in increasing the effectiveness of hiring and selection. Think about it. Hiring the wrong person can cost two and one-half times the person's salary. This was the impetus behind the development of this model. The former Bell System once reported that it interviewed 1 million women annually, it hired 125,000 of them, and yet its net productivity gain was only 15,000 employees. This paradox was the business problem that inspired the Forté solution. Context matters—classic validity and commercial value. Join us now for our interview with the developer of this anatomy, C. D. "Hoop" Morgan, founder and chairman of the Forté Institute in Wilmington, North Carolina.

Bring Out the Best: Tell us, Hoop, because we so often hear the terms used interchangeably, what is the difference between a personality profile and a communication style profile?

Hoop Morgan: A personality profile literally is that; it's an attempt to describe the personal preferences of how someone is, how they like to be treated, or maybe even their interests. It's not aptitudes, aptitudes being natural strengths. Communication style not only deals with the "who I am," but it's the whole concept of how can I put this type of information to use. One of the unique pieces of Forté history is that we've pretty much established that it's not really so much "who you are," but it's "how you learn to adapt" to another that is useful. Personality is pretty much set, but your ability to communicate with others can be and should be adaptive.

Bring Out the Best: Would I be safe in saying that the personality profile talks about "me" and very much describes "me," while a communication profile reflects "me" in reference to how I interact with others—me versus we?

Hoop Morgan: Absolutely. We're safe to say in the communication-style report (I like what you've said here) that instead of "me," it's talking about "we"—how I interact with others. I've never met anyone who was successful who couldn't tell you a number of other people who helped them get there. They can give you the list, they can tell you of their significant mentors; successful people think in terms of *we*.

Another thought to consider is that a personality test is typically a once and done. That's it. Built into a proper communication profile is a metric that portrays how you are adapting—a report with fluidity. You mentioned that our behavioral patterns are generally formed 70 percent by environmental influences, by what happens to us, and only 30 percent by our genetic hardwiring. Forté reflects your "hardwiring" from birth, as well as how you are adapting right now and even how you are most likely coming across to others—how you're being perceived. That's a huge difference.

Bring Out the Best: Hoop, you get the bigger picture with so many thousands of profile reports at your fingertips. In your current work, are there any particular dynamics you're seeing that you'd like to talk about?

Hoop Morgan: We work with all levels of organizations, college students to CEOs, and one of the concerns I've got is the technology lag has created a real gap in terms of people becoming good at perhaps efficiently communicating and not so good at effectively collaborating. You've mentioned so many times the power and necessity of being present with others, to be in the moment. My observation is that it's hard to do that when you're sitting there

115

texting someone while your boss is going over an assignment, and it's regarded as an absolutely normal behavior. In some ways our new technologies may be setting us up for failure. You are so right, not only should the leader be present in the moment, so should the follower!

Bring Out the Best: Hold on a minute and let's look up *collaborate* and *communicate*. To communicate is to impart knowledge, to make known, to communicate information, to give to another, and transmit. Now when I look up collaborate the definition I get is, to work one with another, to cooperate, usually willingly. So *that's* what you're getting at—that difference, and the challenge for us is that there will be a lot of people with the skills to communicate, but not a lot of people with the skills to collaborate—to work with one another.

Hoop Morgan: Yeah, and I mean this is not intentional. One of the phrases you used when looking at communicate was "to transmit," and now we have a whole generation coming up who are masters of transmitting a lot of information electronically yet perhaps without the skill set to sit down and have that type of meaningful, in the moment, in the present one-on-one communication. Extrapolate that out some 30 more years, and if we don't have a course correction, what might be happening then?

Bring Out the Best: With each of our collaborations on different chapters of this book, we've asked our interviewees four key questions, the first being, Hoop, if you could tell tomorrow's leader just one thing, what would it be?

Hoop Morgan: Listen.

Bring Out the Best: For those same leaders of tomorrow, what is the one thing you would tell them to start doing?

Hoop Morgan: Practice situational awareness. It can be focused on any number of things: competency, environment, perception. But become aware of how you're most likely coming across to others. The more acute your situational awareness, the better leader and listener you become. I guess that's another euphemism for your being present.

Bring Out the Best: What would you have them stop doing, Hoop?

Hoop Morgan: Assuming. Acting on input without being curious and questioning. Passing judgment without data.

Bring Out the Best: And your advice to tomorrow's leaders on what to continue doing?

Hoop Morgan: Developing the ability to adapt, to adapt with agility. That doesn't mean just quickly; it means to adapt in the ways that are going to give you the best return on your influence.

Bring Out the Best: One final question, Hoop. I saw on your website the phrase, "the 4 Rs." Tell us about that.

Hoop Morgan: It stands for "reading-(w)riting-(a)rithmetic, and relationships. The saying came from a partnership effort I had with a gentleman by the name of Peter Hershend. He and his brother started Hershend Entertainment. They own Dollywood, Stone Mountain, and the Whitewater theme parks. His way to give back was through his work with education in Missouri. That was where the fourth R came from—adding personal and interpersonal skills to the K–12 environment and beyond for the student and the educator. Peter is a very bright man.

In capping off this chapter, we would like to provide you with a communication-style report, no fees, no strings. You can have the same profiling done that Don had, at no cost at all. We want you to have this first piece of situational awareness. It takes only a few minutes to complete and can make a big difference in how you view yourself and how you view others. It follows the anatomy of communication you've just learned, and all you need to do is go online to: http://www.theforteinstitute.com/FreeRequest/Start.aspx?RefID=19835.

Follow the directions, and eight minutes later the profile is in your inbox. Then come back to the final section in preparing yourself to lead in a no-normal world—the protocol.

SECTION FOUR

THE PROTOCOL

A *protocol* is an accepted code, a prescribed approach for correct conduct or action, a set of conventional principles and expectations. The origin of the word is from the Greek "protokollon" meaning "to glue together." Our objective then for this fourth capstone section is to provide you with the tools you need for effective influence in a no-normal world; the interactional competence to engage, a *leader's* protocol to guide, and the personal fuel to ignite your efforts:

- ○ **Awareness and attention.** Your skill at being present with others is *how* you engage effectively in a no-normal world. Being present builds empathy. Through empathy you engage, and through engagement you build capacity.
- ○ **Making every moment count.** Learn a *leader's* protocol, research-based and real-time workable. Master a leadership model that is designed to equip, not just educate.
- ○ **Energy matters.** Learn from the best how to maintain your passion for the task at hand and the *people* at hand. This is a powerful yet simple approach to building the resilience it takes to lead today and in the years to come.

CHAPTER 8

Awareness and Attention: Learning to Be Present

hat you focus on expands, and you've learned what to focus on—the core of your team. You have studied anatomy, the anatomy of your communication. You've prepared yourself. You're ready now to learn the *how-to* of leading in a no-normal world. In this chapter and the next two chapters you will learn how to immerse yourself in the moment, to master the number-one leadership competency of this era: being present with others. You will discover how to adopt a leader's protocol to meet your need for output and your team's need for connection. Finally, we'll show you how to find the energy you need to do it all: be present with others, establish a real-time protocol, and build the personal resilience it takes to handle the intensity of leading today. This is millennial leadership.

Over the years we've had the good fortune to work with some of the top thought leaders in the world of management. We know that a leader's job has always been to create readiness in those he or she is responsible for. The challenge too has always been to replicate the results of effective leaders. Early on, there was a school of thought, a "trait" phase, in which all our best efforts centered on what kind of person made an effective leader—the "born leader." The traits or attributes of successful leaders were studied, and the search was on for how to best hire the people who had these traits and attitudes. A subsequent approach, a behavioral phase, then brought about the idea that if we could only isolate the behaviors that effective leaders engage in, we could then teach other leaders to mimic them. Finally, contingencies inspired a new way to try to increase our odds. Several diagnostic or situational models of leadership were the high-probability approach of their day.

All these approaches have merit and power in developing readiness to perform. They also each had their genesis in the business dynamics of their day. What about *our* day? We believe that the business climate today is different. We believe that the dynamics of creating capacity without headcount in the second and third decades of the new millennium demand a new paradigm, a new frame of reference, and a new way to develop and maintain capacity. So what is different about today? What is it about human interactions in leadership today that is different from what it was 10, 20, or 50 years ago? In a word, *time*.

There was a wonderful presentation given by David M. Levy, a professor at the University of Washington, called "No Time to Think." Professor Levy's premise was that we are losing our capacity for deeper thought and reflection because of the pace of living and working in the twenty-first century. We would like to take a giant step forward and reinforce what we began in Chapter 2. We are losing our capacity not only for reflection but also for connection. Far more critical to the world of leadership is the idea that *there is no time to be.* We find that our collective concept of time is accelerating and fragmenting to the point where, if we let it, the urgent would crowd out the important.

122

The State of the Moment

Do you find yourself all too often on autopilot? Do you forget a name immediately after you first meet someone? Does it take extraordinary amounts of time to recognize physical tension in your own body? Do you move in a rush from one task to the next? Do you experience a variety of emotions without being aware of them? Do you drop or spill items on a regular basis without knowing why?

These are signs that you are having difficulty in *being present*—the state of being aware of and attentive to what is taking place in the moment. Do you know that on a scale of 1 to 6, most people average around 3.5 when it comes to this skill of intentional consciousness? And it is a skill, one that can be sharpened or dulled by a variety of factors. It is a skill that pays dividends, both personal and professional. In our personal lives the capacity to be present is strongly correlated with lower levels of self-absorption, depression, anger, anxiety, hostility, and impulsiveness and with higher levels of happiness and well-being. Professionally, there is a direct relationship between being able to reside in the moment while interacting with others and self-regulation. By striving to be present in our professional lives, we foster the ability to manage destructive interpersonal urges such as interrupting and ignoring others. Perhaps most important to a leader, the ability to be present is directly related to the skills of emotional intelligence and some aspects of social desirability. Leading today is no longer about the state of the relationship. Think instead about the state of the *moment*. The state of the moment involves developing a competency for being present with your people and with yourself. It demands acting on purpose in real time with those who are important to you.

We've been asked many times during workshops to relay what we personally try to embody, what one thing about leading *we* would impart to participants above all else. We respond with, *learn to be present*. Welcome to millennial leadership.

Awareness and Attention

At its most basic, being present is a function of two variables: awareness and attention. Let's start with an operational definition of each.

Awareness is being informed of current developments, which is a function of conscious perception or sensitivity. As one half of what it takes to be present, awareness is the front-runner. While it might be in the background of thought, a scanning function for gathering information, you *can* be aware of something without necessarily paying attention to it. You won't always think about the items that lie within the scope of your awareness, but you do often scan them. You can be consciously looking for items of interest, generally with low levels of intensity. When they show up, they grab your attention, and the intensity of your interest rises.

Attention is a focused awareness, a narrowing of consciousness and a directing of the mind, concentration, and fixation. Attention is built upon the foundation of awareness. Paying attention involves the focusing and strengthening of the intensity of our conscious awareness. We've been aware of it, and now we're noticing it. Attention brings the subject from background to foreground, from peripheral thought to central thought. It is a heightened sensitivity to a more limited number of items, perhaps just *one* intense experience within our awareness. That is attention.

The whole idea of mindfulness, then, as opposed to mindlessness, is all about conscious, purposeful awareness and attention. Being present is just that: single-mindedly being aware of and attentive to what is taking place *in* the present. We have a saying that there are only three real time zones—past, present, and future. Being present with others means residing in the present tense. Where do you live? We know that we won't always be in the moment. We do need to spend some alone time to learn from the past. We need that same opportunity to plan for the future. Yet what happens when you spend too much time in the past? What will you experience? Depression. What happens when you spend too much time somewhere out in the future? Anxiety. Most importantly for our work here, what happens when you *aren't* alone, and, for whatever reason, you've left "present standard time"? It's the number-one empathy killer—the inability to be present, *to pay attention to* the person you are interacting with. This is what makes other people feel that you don't understand or care about their experience. Does it matter *why* we aren't present with someone else? Let us be clear. No, it doesn't. While we believe that the pressures of time and technology have a great deal to do with it, understanding is important only to acceptance. We would submit that we all accept the importance of paying attention to the people we interact with. Forget about rationalizing when you don't. Just focus on developing the ability to do better next time.

The Mindful Attention and Awareness Scale (MAAS)

The work of two people has established a powerful legitimacy to the impact of being present by measuring our ability to do so. Kirk Warren Brown and Richard M. Ryan are two researchers at the University of Rochester who have designed and validated an assessment called the Mindful Attention and Awareness Scale. What appears to be a simple 15-item questionnaire began as a pool of 184 items reflecting intellectual, emotional, physical, interpersonal, or general tendencies to be present with others. After a long validation process, the result is a simple questionnaire that indeed *quantifies* how mindful or present you are able to be.

There are two important points we'd like to make in relation to the MAAS assessment:

1. **Find out for yourself.** There is a copy of the instrument in the Appendix. Take a few minutes when you're finished reading this to turn to the Appendix and complete the assessment. It is a collection of 15 statements about your everyday experience. Using the 1 to 6 scale, just check how frequently or infrequently you currently experience each item. It's as simple as that. Answer according to what *really reflects* your experience rather than what you think it should be. Treat each item separately. To score the assessment, add all your scores and divide by 15 to give you a mean score of "dispositional mindfulness" or your ability to be present. The average is around three and a half. This number is not only derived from the original research of Brown and Ryan, but it's also been confirmed by our own participants. This is one of the few self-assessments in which the average score often goes *down*—it gets worse—once participants discover the power of being present. The more they learn, the more they realize how mindless they have become. Take a few minutes to find out how good *you* are at being present.

2. **Understand the return.** We also want to reiterate the power of dispositional mindfulness—of being present. Brown and Ryan and others have not only validated the assessment, meaning that they've proven that it does in fact measure what it claims to, but they've also correlated being present with other psychological constructs. In other words, they have shown the connections between the ability to be present and all kinds of personal well-being. The better you are at being present, the less depressed, anxious, hostile, or impulsive you will be. The better you are at being present with others, the better you are at being *happy* with yourself. The more successful you are at increasing dispositional mindfulness, the better you are at controlling yourself. We call it self-regulation. It means that with being present comes the ability to control ourselves and not rudely interrupt others as much as we might otherwise. When mindfulness

goes up, so does social desirability. In short, you become more *likable*.

Take a few minutes now. Go to the Appendix and complete the MAAS instrument. Find out how present you are capable of being. Discover how mindful you are on a regular basis. Then come back here to learn how to *increase* your capacity to be aware and pay attention.

Cultivate Capacity and Frequency

There are two ways to go about getting better at dispositional mindfulness. One is through growing your personal capacity, that is, increasing your ability. The other is some sort of frequency increase. In one case you become better at being present; in the other you just strive to be in the moment more often. We do not advocate one approach or the other. In our last book with Marshall Goldsmith, *What Got You Here Won't Get You There—in Sales!*, we agreed that in personal growth we give awards for starting and running the race rather than finishing it. We're not even sure where the finish line is. What we have crafted for you here is a powerful top-20 set of suggestions; 20 action verbs with explanations of specifically what to do to either get better at being present or to increase the likelihood that you will pay attention more often. It's as simple as that— simple, but never easy. As always, the rule of three applies! Pick three suggestions that resonate with you, three that make sense to you, three that seem to be something you think you could realistically take on. That's all. You'll be amazed at the results you can achieve:

1. *Activate* **your five senses.** Look for opportunities to engage your sense of smell, taste, touch, sight, or hearing. We mention in Chapter 2 that our brains work off of two distinct circuits:

default and direct. The default circuit is just that, the one that kicks in when not much is happening. This circuit is a running litany of self-talk. Some call it the narrative circuit, and the only voice you hear is your own. In fact, during any given interaction, it's almost a coin toss as to whether you or the people you're talking with are actively listening. The direct circuit is activated when our senses take in data. It's the circuit of the present moment. Purposely engaging any one of your senses brings you into the present. And the two circuits of your brain, the default and direct, are inversely correlated. This means that when one kicks in, the other kicks out. You have a choice. The default circuit is fine for planning, considering, visioning. The direct circuit is your pathway to interactions. Choose your direct circuit; activate your senses.

2. *Approach* **those you interact with.** We mean this both literally and figuratively. Our brains are always assessing others as to friend or foe. This isn't conscious. Your brain is constantly judging whether or not another person is a threat, and in the absence of data, your brain will go with threat. The simple fact of your being somcone's boss automatically *raises* tension in employees. It automatically moves you into the threat category in their brain. Have you ever looked to see whether you attract or repel those around you? Our advice here is to try to approach others, especially as their leader. Your position of power often creates separation you're not aware of.

3. *Audit* **your "CPA."** With thanks to this chapter's interviewee, Terri Egan at Pepperdine University, your CPA is your continuous partial attention, your almost radar-like scanning of what goes on around you. In our discussions with Terri she strongly recommended that you audit this radar to get an idea of what you then tend to be distracted by. What is *your* temptation of choice when your mind wanders off from one subject to the next? Our distracters tend to be identifiable and consistent.

For you, are they thoughts of certain people, after-hours activities, looming deadlines? If we can identify them, we can manage them. If you can name it, you can tame it.

4. *Befriend* **those you meet and those you know.** Get to know another person, anytime, anyplace. Find out who people are, what they like, what they *are* like. Don't worry that your interest isn't always reciprocated. No worries that you may never see the person again. This is definitely a two-for-one. In most cases all it takes is to engage another person in light conversation, and 10 minutes are plenty. This person will perceive that you understand and care. You reinforce the empathic connection. And the second benefit? Your brain will function more efficiently; you will get better at what you do. It's proven that engaging in brief social contact boosts executive function, your working memory, and your ability to self-monitor. Purposeful small talk engages your target and sharpens your interactional skills. Try it.

5. *Breathe* **one count in, two counts out.** Interacting consumes significant amounts of energy. Where does your body get energy on a moment-to-moment basis? *Oxygen* rules! In fact, our brains use a tremendous amount of blood flow, which in turn consumes oxygen. Deep breathing is a high-value strategy in that it usually engages your senses in some way as well. It also provides an unintended time out for everyone—just a moment or two where the person doing the deep breathing won't be speaking. Take oxygen in and let it out. If you read up at all on running, the advice is always to breathe out twice as long as you breathe in for maximum results. One count in, two counts out. And if it's a really rough interpersonal "marathon," tilt your head back to open up your airways and open your mouth to take in even more volume of air. Too many times when conversations get intense, we forget to breathe, we lose energy, and we lose focus.

6. *Cancel* **the meeting.** (Again, thanks to our conversations with Terri Egan for this one.) Stop having meetings that don't focus on the relationships among the people you're meeting with. Every face-to-face meeting today should have at its core something that's going to foster a deeper personal connection between the parties present. If it doesn't, stop wasting everyone's time. This is one of the biggest disconnects of the no-normal world. Who doesn't complain about meetings that go nowhere, accomplish nothing, and take people away from doing their jobs? We are busier than we have ever been in our lives. If you are going to hold the meeting, make it about the souls in attendance.

7. *Condition* **your physical being.** Rest, diet, and exercise play more of a part in your ability to effectively interact with others than you might imagine. Pulling a professional all-nighter, putting in 70-hour work weeks, or burning the candle at both ends (for the good of the organization) is still viewed as a positive sign of commitment and loyalty. Yet what's the cost? What kind of diminishing returns are there? What do we lose when we ignore the needs of our body for the needs of the enterprise? We all know that taking care of ourselves pays dividends; we just don't normally consider the toll it can take on our relationships. The less we care for ourselves, the less we are able to care for others. Believe it.

8. *Dedicate* **time and attention to those you are with.** This means verbally, overtly, and obviously pledging the moment in time to them. It may seem obvious that if you're sitting down together, the time is theirs. Don't assume your interaction partners know this. What do you have to lose by being obvious about your intent? In fact, extend the idea of verbalizing the intent of the time together to also verbalizing your attempts at being as present as humanly possible with them for the time that you have together. Say to them that this time

belongs to them and mean it. Say to them, "I am trying to do better at paying attention to the people I am with." We find that the obvious often isn't all that obvious. Whether or not it should be obvious doesn't really matter, does it? Don't worry about verbal redundancy. In dedicating time to someone, everyone wins.

9. *Disconnect* **from annoying technology.** This seems obvious as well, doesn't it? Yet we don't do it. We believe (and hope) that several years from now the inconsiderate texting, surfing, or e-mailing that people do while they're engaged in conversation will be no more acceptable than lighting up a cigarette is today. Designate technology-free zones and technology-free times. We know of many families that half-heartedly decree, "No phones at the dinner table," only to lack conviction and consistency in enforcement. Set some rules. Follow these rules when it comes to the use of technology. Is it okay to take notes on a laptop during meetings instead of using pen and paper? Probably. Is it also okay to leave your Outlook open too so you can respond to e-mail, IM, or even check Facebook while you're taking notes? Is it okay to correspond via e-mail while you're on the phone with someone else? If you care at all about being present, the answer to these questions is *no*.

10. *Formalize* **your communication practices.** As you would for a new reporting system, a new CRM, or a staff reorganization, put the weight of legitimacy behind your leadership protocol. Put it in writing. Communicate it to all those involved. If you decide to leave iPhones out of meetings from now on, publish it. If you decide to designate a certain conference room as tech-free, put the word out. Treat your decisions about interaction as you would any other tactical move. Use more than one message, more than one medium and document in whatever method you need to make it stick.

11. *Measure* **the quality of your interactions.** We have a saying: "If you can measure it, you can change it." We know from our coaching practice that you can *enlist* the help of those who matter to you. *Ask* them to rate the effectiveness of your attempts at interpersonal improvement and *accept* their input to guide future interactions. A simple e-mail once a month is all it takes. Ask two or three key individuals to rate your ability to be present when you interact with them. Ask them to score your attempts at paying attention during conversations, from minus 3 (significantly worse) to plus 3 (significantly better). That's all. Nothing more complicated. If you can measure it, you can change it.

12. *Mirror* **the response you want to see.** We spoke before of the power of our brains and what are called *mirror neurons.* In essence, our brains react the same (they light up) whether we execute or we simply watch someone else execute. The same pathways in our gray matter carry the signals for both doing and observing. What happens when you see someone yawn? You yawn also. What happens when someone walks up to you smiling? You immediately feel the pull of your own smile begin. The message here is to stop before you meet. Take a moment to put your game face on. In a tense athletic competition, the image you project might be one of unrelenting drive and will to win. When you meet with one of your people, what image do you want to project? The emotions you project will find physiological resonance in the minds of those you interact with. Part of being present is preparing for the role.

13. *Narrow* **the scope of your intentions.** Research over the last 60 years started with a conclusion that we could keep up to seven ideas in mind, juggle seven tasks. That number came down to four with further study, and now the literature shows that the number of tasks we can handle at once, without degradation of effectiveness, is one. We can multitask, but with

each additional item added, our performance goes down. This profound conclusion applies to when we are alone and *multiplies* when we're not alone. To do a better job of being present, narrow your scope. Reduce the number of action items to cover, or at a bare minimum tackle them one at a time.

14. *Notice* **the impact you have.** Warren Bennis in his powerful work *On Becoming a Leader* (Perseus Books, 1989) advised that we all become "first-class noticers." Although his context was slightly different, we know that noticing matters. Noticing strengthens connections in your brain. Noticing reinforces results, good and bad. When you have the impact you intend with someone, stop and notice it. Mentally acknowledge it. Conversely, when the effect you have is not what you wanted, take the time to notice that, too. Whether his or her face lights up or quickly goes dark, don't look away. *Notice* the impact you have in your attempts to be present with others.

15. *Personalize* **your conversation.** There's an old saying that everyone's favorite sound is that of their own name. The idea of self-representation starts at one year of age. We recognize ourselves. We recognize sights and *sounds* that represent *us*. There is significant acceleration of activity in several parts of our brains at the sound of our first name. We engage other people's brains when we speak their name. They can't help it; they're not conscious of it; the light goes on. When you meet someone for the first time and would like to remember his or her name (hard, isn't it?), the most powerful tip is to repeat that name three times to yourself and twice aloud as you go through the introductions. Whatever method you use, twice out loud and three times to yourself while *looking* at that person. This association serves to engage you both in being present. The payback is powerful, and don't save the technique only for new introductions. Try it with someone you already know. Find a reason to say their name aloud twice and

three times to yourself. You'll engage, the other person will engage, and you both get a good start at staying present with each other.

16. *Reboot* **your interpersonal RAM.** The area of your brain known as the PFC or prefrontal cortex, we've come to describe as your interpersonal RAM. Computers have what is called random access memory (RAM). Current applications, operating systems, and programs are all accessed through RAM, and you can tell when a computer is trying to do too much at once. What happens? It slows down or even freezes. It locks up. Our own interpersonal RAM operates much the same way. Our PFC is what we use to store information we need now, what we need to interact right now. What happens when we overload it? We slow down; we get sloppy or lazy or simply freeze up. When you find yourself overloading on tasks or interaction, reboot. With a computer we just shut it down and turn it back on again to clear the RAM. What does it take to help you reboot? Perhaps put a conversation on hold. Agree to revisit at a point in the future. Go for a short walk, get a cup of tea, take a few deep breaths—whatever it takes for you to reboot and start up again. It's not a failure. It's not defeat. It is just a short delay.

17. *Schedule* **regular, intentional, daily interaction.** The military services in every corner of the world place a high value on personal *physical* performance and schedule its development daily. Physical training, or PT, is a part of the daily ritual of millions of people around the world. To become and stay physically fit takes daily commitment and repetition. To become "interactionally" fit takes the same commitment and repetition. Don't wait. Become fit now. Put it in your Outlook. Set aside time for interaction, even if it's just for 15 minutes. Much the way we look forward to a workout or a run, we

begin to eagerly anticipate the interpersonal workout as well. Schedule one every day.

18. *Study* **for its own sake.** Understanding brings change. As you learn, your thoughts change. As your thoughts change, so does your brain, quite literally. Establish a mechanism through which you can continue to learn and grow. The entire world is at your fingertips through the Internet. Once a week, set aside a 15- to 30-minute segment in which you will study some aspect of interaction or interpersonal communication. Most of us do so in reference to our functional, clinical, or legal knowledge. Continuing education is not a new concept, yet with respect to how we interact with others, the semester never even starts. Change that practice. Become a student of interaction. Become a first-class studier as well as a first-class noticer.

19. *Substitute* **a new route or routine.** Changing any habit, even a healthy one, can heighten your awareness, and that's halfway to being present. As we follow the same routine day in and day out, we dull our awareness. We travel on autopilot. Do you take a long drive to work and can't remember a single minute of the commute? Change the route. Change your breakfast. Change your customary dress code for the day. It will key up a heightened sense of presence, of being there. Give it a try.

20. *Silence* **the auditory interrupters.** Your auditory interrupters may be the television at home or in the hotel room, the radio in the car, the sound of the engines on an airliner. Take steps to find a short, quiet respite from the noise. Earplugs on the plane. Leaving the sound off on the TV (yes, you can leave the set on; just use the mute button). Driving in peace. You all know that quiet time is effective with children of a certain age. They come out of their room with a different *outlook* on life. Give yourself the same pause, the same few minutes of quiet every day. It's even more effective when you aren't forced to do it.

We hope you profit from these 20 suggestions. Take your time. Adopt three of them as part of your new leadership protocol. Right now get ready for a powerful interview on the art and science of being present with Dr. Terri Egan.

A nationally recognized management scholar and speaker, Terri Egan is an associate professor of applied behavioral science at Pepperdine University's Graziadio School of Business and Management, and director of the top-ranked masters of science in organization development program. Terri shares our passion for the power of being present and its applications to the very specific context of effective leadership.

Bring Out the Best: Welcome, Terri. If you were to describe your area of training or your area of focus and expertise, how would you define it?

Terri Egan: My area of study is helping people understand how to develop the capacity in themselves and others to reach the results that they most desire. In doing that, I believe that we have to fully understand the complexity of who we all are as human beings. The new discoveries about how the mind and brain work offer a platform to help us move into much greater capacity overall. A lot of what we used to believe were limits on people's ability have now been removed because we understand the way the mind and the brain interact.

Bring Out the Best: Given that, when you talk about what we know about how the mind and brain work, what's different today? What do we know now that we didn't know five years ago?

Terri Egan: What we know now is that the brain is plastic, and we can use our focused attention to reshape neural pathways to create the conditions to shape our own behavior and biology. We're no longer victims of our past, our circumstances, or our environment. A lot of what we've been able to learn is a function of the changes in technology that allow us to see changes in the brain—in people who are living. This is an area where technology has really been our friend, and functional MRI (magnetic resonance imaging) allows us to understand changes that in the past we could only guess at, but couldn't understand fully.

Bring Out the Best: With so much change through the use of imaging technology, what could be next? What is going to be different? Right now we're four or five years into the infancy of applying some of this to the understanding of leadership and influence. What's going to be different in five to ten more years?

Terri Egan: Imaging technology aside, I think there are three potential areas that could be quite different. One is that the people we're leading are going to be different. The young people who are coming into our organizations will have grown up with a very different set of ways in how they relate to each other and to authority. I read an interesting editorial in the *Wall Street Journal* that talked about the potential negative impact of people engaged in so much social media that they are not engaged face to face. What we know about mirror neurons is that it's not just body language that we pick up on when we're interacting that tells us whether someone is paying attention or someone cares about us, but there's actually a physiological change that is picked up in our brain that allows us to tune into what other people are thinking and feeling, and to read that and experience it as if we were experiencing it ourselves. The article was pointing out that as we move into fewer face-to-face encounters, those mirror neurons and the ways they relate, they actually become less activated. This means reduced degrees of compassion, empathy, connection, and understanding. It tracks with your research, and I don't know about you, but it causes me to be concerned.

137

We really don't understand the long-term implications of the increase in social media. We know that someone who has grown up with a lot of access to social media and computing can switch applications much more quickly than someone who had to learn that at a later age. So the good thing is that a younger person can perhaps multitask more efficiently. However, when it comes to more complex problem solving and connecting through compassion and empathy with human beings, that doesn't necessarily carry forward.

I think another difference we've got to contend with is that because we have fewer resources overall to use in organizations, we're going to have to consider more of our internal resources as precious. Meaning our well-being—our *physical* well-being.

Bring Out the Best: Creating capacity without headcount.

Terri Egan: Exactly, and to make that happen, I think we'll see a resurgence in organizations paying attention to well-being. Right now we see people paying attention to metrics, but the real question is, will more attention be paid to helping people be healthier? You would be laughed off of any stage if you proposed that a three-martini lunch was a good idea, now. Right? Yet we have people who consider it a badge of honor to work late, work long, and get very little sleep. And yet we know, science shows us, that sleep deprivation has an impact similar to alcohol.

The final dynamic would certainly be the increase in demands on our attention, and making it difficult for people to really be disciplined, because of the increase in technology. There is a "Twitter curve" that has the adoption of technology on the left side, beginning with cell phones going up to Facebook, and on the bottom there's the time between interruptions. We could go for hours without interruption in the 1980s, to virtually nothing today. This will have an effect.

138

Bring Out the Best: Terri, how about our discussions about what to do to increase our abilities in being present with others, or at least increase the odds that we will pay attention to them? Is there anything we missed?

Terri Egan: Perhaps just the idea to take time every day to be inspired. This might mean spending time with a pet, or for you and me, Don, with our horses or our families. Time with music, with art, with our hobbies or pastimes. We know that what activates a sense of joy and happiness is also a resource we can draw from in being present with others. There is no leadership competency more important than being present today, and our mood is contagious. If we can find ways to be inspired, engaged, and happy, it's going to be easier to be in that state with other people. It also gives us something to shift to and draw from when we're feeling tired, frustrated, or irritated. How much time do you spend during the day in activities that are frustrating and irritating versus those that are energizing, fun, and inspiring? That is a choice we can teach people to make.

Bring Out the Best: Terri, there are four questions that we like to ask in closing of all our interviews. We have 6,000 answers to them, and we'd like to add your wisdom to the mix. If you could tell people just one thing about their leadership, what would it be?

Terri Egan: Pay attention, now.

Bring Out the Best: What would you tell them to start doing?

Terri Egan: Be selfish with your own time. It matters.

Bring Out the Best: And is there anything they should stop or continue doing?

Terri Egan: To continue doing. I think as your research for this book pointed out, there's something important about the work that you do and the connection with the people you love. I would say to continue to find out what's working and amplify that. It could even be the person you find most challenging to deal with. There is something about that person that's okay. Find that and focus on it. Continue building on what's working well during the day. Find the things that you *do* appreciate, and put your attention on them. That's more than enough.

Awareness and attention. Your skill at being present with others is *how* you engage effectively in a no-normal world. Being present builds empathy. Through empathy you engage, and through engagement you build capacity without adding headcount.

Now let's move on to learn the *leader's* protocol—research-based and real-time executable. In the next chapter we discuss a leadership model that is designed to equip, not just educate—to make every leading moment count.

CHAPTER 9

The Leader's Protocol: Making Every Moment Count

As with most people in leadership or managerial roles today, there is an abundance of structure in place for the management side of the job. Policies, procedures, performance management, processes, approvals, scheduling, forecasting—it's a job just to *comply* with it all. And how engaging (for you *or* your team members) is that side of what you do every day?

Let's look at the leadership side of your job. We define *leadership* as simply bringing out the best in those who matter to you, *and* bringing out the best in yourself while you're at it. What kind of structure or design does your employer put in place for the *human* interactions you engage in on its behalf? Our experience (and our research) tells us that the answer to how much guidance you get is not much. In many organizations, it approaches zero.

So what we offer you is a *leader's* protocol. We define protocol at the beginning of Section Four as being a code of behavior or correct conduct or action. Within these pages you get the proven principles and expectations for a *leader's* conduct, a model for effective leadership in a no-normal world, based on solid, current, global research. In reading on you get the structure you need for making the most of every moment.

Foundational Assumptions

As we dig into a capstone chapter like this (this one can be *pivotal* to your leadership career), we like to first check our foundational assumptions. An assumption by its nature is something that we accept or hold true *without* proof, demonstration, or even consideration. When it comes to unveiling a powerful leadership model, we want you to be consciously aware of what's behind our thinking:

○ **Assumption 1: What we present is based upon scientific process.** We mean that we are applying the results of quantitative research. What we offer you is not supposition, guesswork, or hopeful reckoning. It seems to us that regardless of organizational level, the most prevalent method of becoming a more effective leader is through making mistakes, and this can be a very costly approach. We would like to tip the balance of that equation for you. We offer what we know to be true. *It's already tested.* Trust it.

○ **Assumption 2: There is a bottom-line return on leadership. Leadership is not just "nice to know about."** Go back to the concepts of human asset accounting. The condition of your human resources carries real value: the consensus is approximately *twice current payroll.* If your team's annual payroll is three quarters of a million dollars, then it carries an asset value of $1.5 million. We've seen far too many examples of organizations taking the short-sighted strategy of liquidating human assets in the name of shareholder value, eliminating people and claiming increased profit. Adopting a model of influence that gets the results you need, while improving the engagement of the core of your team, can return very real dollars to the enterprise.

○ **Assumption 3: Leadership takes place in the moment.** This is a tool for real-time influence interactions, outbound or inbound, planned or unplanned. We submit that most are unplanned today, yet we need to be as effective as if our interactions were a scheduled quarterly review. This protocol is targeted specifically to the needs of no-normal operations: resilient, adaptable, effective, even in the moment.

○ **Assumption 4: There is a difference between model and theory.** This is a personal nod to the teachings of a mentor of one of your authors and one of the last living gurus of the applied behavioral sciences, Paul Hersey. While a theory can explain why a method succeeds or fails, a model allows you to replicate success. We offer you a leader's protocol: a *model* for correct conduct or action, based on scientific method, built to effect a measurable return for you and your organization by making every leadership moment count.

Scientific Process: The Survey Base

We've built this leadership protocol on the foundation of scientific process: over 6,000 survey responses from all over the globe, analyzed manually and through text analytics, with answers loud and clear and in a powerfully consistent category sequence—*communication, praise and recognition, treatment and respect, performance review,* and *independence.* These are the needs of your followers. We're not guessing at this. We asked the employees who responded to the survey what they need, and they told us. Being believers of our own doctrine, we applied the rule of three and streamlined their responses into a powerful triad that you can use to understand what's required of any leadership moment: communication, feedback, autonomy.

143

Your most powerful consideration of what core team members want on any given day? Communication. Talk to them! What do they need next? Feedback. How are they doing? And the final in-the-moment diagnostic? Autonomy. Who owns the work, and how closely does the leader need to be involved? This protocol, these three dynamics working in concert, gives you the best chance of crafting an effective leadership moment and making it count. Let's take each one separately and display it in a way that you can use, real-time, every time. (See Figure 9.1.)

FIGURE **9.1** **Complete Protocol Model**

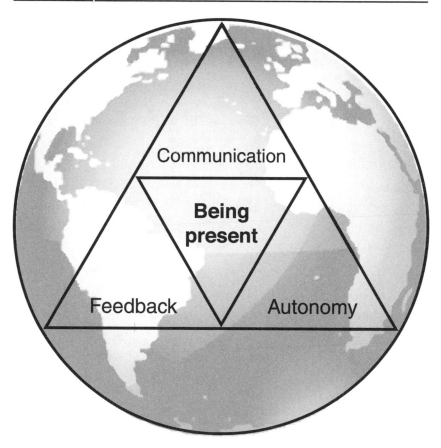

The Leader's Protocol

What you see in Figure 9.1 replicates what happens in an effective influence interaction—an anatomy of the moment. The key leadership competency of being present with others is surrounded by the followers' needs for communication, feedback, and autonomy. Notice it, plan it, measure it. All we have to do is be present to understand what someone needs from us in terms of communication, feedback, and autonomy. It is simple, but not easy. Executing this in a no-normal world of interruptions, technology, and

FIGURE 9.2   Communication: Purpose and Style

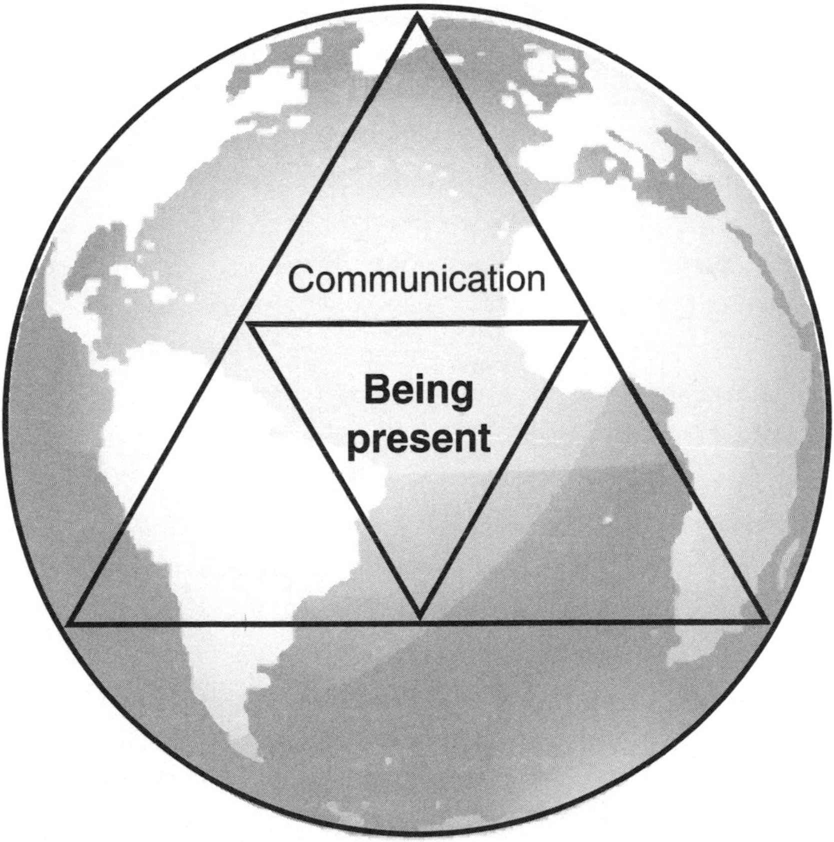

organizational upheaval is challenging. We spent a whole chapter together on how to build your skill set at being present. Now let's dissect each of the needs that revolve around you. If you can understand employees' needs, you can respond in a manner that has the best chance of engaging their discretionary effort and creating new capacity.

1. Communication: Purpose and Style

We asked thousands of people from Singapore to Syracuse four simple questions around the number-one thing they would say to their bosses about their leadership, and what they wanted their bosses to stop, start, and continue doing in leading them. Far and away the most common response centered on communication (Figure 9.2). Your job now is using what you now know *in the moment*. Just as healthcare workers maintain their professional protocol with patients, you too have a professional *leadership* protocol to adhere to. Your first consideration when someone knocks on your office door and asks, "You got a minute?" is understanding what communication needs exist right at that moment with this particular person. Here are the two questions that our research shows will help you do it:

1. What is the *purpose* of my communication?
2. What *style* of communication would be most effective?

Purpose

There are few things more frustrating than walking into a room and forgetting why you're there (come on, you can admit you've done it). You first waste time in aimless wandering, and then you compound the sin with a futile attempt to recall your purpose. How about when you involve a second party? You find yourself communicating with one of your people, but if pressed, you can't articulate the conversation's purpose or agenda. How many precious moments do we waste every day with rudderless chatter? There are really only three reasons to communicate. Try using the following to set a target before you speak:

- **Communicating to relate—to establish or maintain association.** In this case, relax, respect whatever social rituals are appropriate to your setting, take turns talking and listening, leave enough time for it, and find the right spot if you can.
- **Communicating to influence—to sway or have some desired effect on another person.** This takes establishing, persuading, and reinforcing (in that order). Make sure you know where you arc in that sequence.
- **Communicating to inform—to transfer knowledge or simply provoke awareness.** First, get your data straight (check your facts), translate those data into what they mean to the people you're talking to, and then check to make sure they understand.

Style

When you have a purpose guiding the moment, the question becomes, What *style* of communication will then be most effective? The easiest taxonomy to use in the moment is one you've already learned: extrovert versus introvert. Just consider whether the person you're communicating with is extroverted or introverted. We like to say that introverts like to think before they speak and that extroverts always speak while they think. Our survey responses were rife with imbalance of this sort. When you have two people conversing, one an introvert and the other an extrovert, and both are blissfully oblivious to the mismatch, the extrovert is thinking, "What's wrong *now*? She isn't saying a word," and the introvert is thinking, "Won't he *ever* stop talking?"

Avoid wasting perfectly good moments this way. Following are some descriptor cues you might use as indicators of another person's communication style (Thanks again to the work of Hoop Morgan):

○ **Introverted.** Private, earnest, reserved, contemplative, quiet, creative, serious, guarded, introspective, secretive, withdrawn, reclusive, aloof

○ **Extroverted.** Enthusiastic, optimistic, humorous, articulate, friendly, eager, fluent, exciting, persuasive, demonstrative, magnetic, annoying, intrusive

FIGURE **9.3**   **Feedback: Process and Praise**

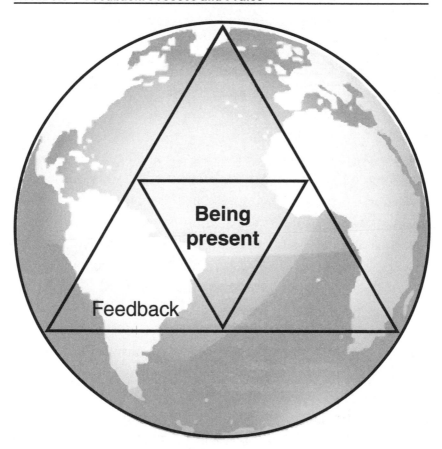

Effective communication revolves around first understanding your purpose and then adapting your style to best understand and be understood. This doesn't take years of study. It takes just a moment of dispositional awareness, of paying attention to another person, making a diagnosis, and *mirroring* what you see. If you're talking to an introvert, try being a little quieter yourself. If that person is an extrovert, open up just a bit. As Doc Hersey used to say, the great thing about the behavioral sciences is that you don't have to be exact. You just have to get close.

Communication is perhaps the most important protocol for leading in the moment. It lies in being aware of and attentive to the communication needs of your followers. Understand *your* purpose. Adapt to *their* style.

2. Feedback: Process and Praise

The research is clear. Your people want to know how they're doing. They want to know what *you* think. They want feedback. They want it from you. Think of feedback as an evaluative response or reaction; your people want that response from you. They want your reaction. They want your *evaluation* of their contribution. When you're in the moment, the quality of your communication matters. It matters first. Next in the equation is your perspective, your take on the moment. The question to you in relation to feedback is, do you provide praise or process (Figure 9.3)? Is your focus esteem or performance? Confidence or technique? Being a leader in the moment doesn't allow for a crowded agenda. Make a choice. Without any implied priority, we take a look at process first.

Process

When you're acknowledging process, three words are relevant in the moment: quality, quantity, and time.

Quality is a factor of performance: is performance meeting expectation or specification? With respect to what brings you and your employee together right now, in this moment, how does their performance meet with your expectations? Maybe even more important, how does it correlate with the expectations or specifications of your ultimate customer?

Quantity always invokes a number, a metric. In considering a quantitative measure of employees' output, is the number low, lagging, moderate, acceptable, high, benchmark or even role model? Is their goal made or missed? Is their work inconsistent or consistent?

Time is a reflection of performance with respect to deadlines. Your diagnostics here should tell you whether your employees are the first to deliver or the last. Are they early or late with product in hand? Have you established expectations as to time frames? Have you communicated your sense of urgency or lack of it? And when you have communicated it, do your employees delight or disappoint you?

If you've made the call that process will outweigh praise right now in *this* moment, then ask yourself *quality, quantity,* or *time*? Don't make it more complex than that. This is a model to use in the moment, and feedback should be transitional, bridging past, present, and future. Accepting the past, adapting to the present toward performing in the future. If it's not about process, then think praise.

Praise

When offering praise, three words are relevant in the moment: effort, contribution, and growth.

Effort is about energy—intensity, power, vigor, exertion. If you are going to praise employees right now in this moment, your first focus should be their effort. Should you be thanking them for going above and beyond? Acknowledging how hard they've been at it? Highlighting the obvious levels of commitment or discipline reflected in their work? Effort is your first focus of praise.

FIGURE 9.4   Autonomy: Ownership and Exit Strategy

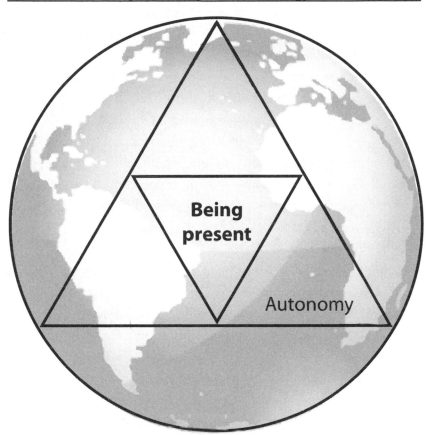

Contribution is about results. Praise focused on contribution can acknowledge superior levels of output, or it can also reflect the positive impact people had upon the performance of others on the team. Praise centered on contribution can also articulate recognition of an individual's part in attaining a larger goal, either the team's or the parent organization's goal.

Growth is about improvement. Praise related to improvement should applaud incremental gain. Development beyond past levels of achievement or seemingly transformational results is at the heart of praise centered on growth.

Second only to effective, meaningful communication, people want feedback. They really do want to know what we think (unlike perhaps lots of people in other parts of our lives). For a leader's protocol of feedback that works in the moment, we need to make one call—do we focus on process or praise? Not both. Pick one and deliver it. You are the one to make that determination. You know the people; you know their work. We know the dynamics of a healthy protocol. For providing feedback, ask yourself where your "moment" is best spent—on quality, quantity, and time, or on their effort, contribution, and growth. If you can be present to ask yourself the question, we know you'll make the right call.

3. Autonomy: Degree of Ownership and Exit Strategy

The last element of follower need in a leader's protocol is autonomy. Over and over, in every corner of the globe—Asia, the Americas, Africa, Europe, the Middle East—followers care about independence, individual responsibility, and freedom to make decisions. Just behind communication and feedback, indicators of autonomy weigh heavily on the minds of your team members. Central to your moment-to-moment adaptive efforts, then, are two very important concepts: ownership and exit (Figure 9.4). What is *their* degree of ownership of the task or objective, and what is *your* exit strategy? Clarity and transparency around these two variables not only engages and maximizes employees' discretionary effort, but they help to free you up as a resource at the same time.

Degree of Ownership

The age-old leadership question is, should the work be leader-driven or follower-driven? Who should make significant decisions? You or your people? When should you let them take the reins, and when should you maintain control? Are they capable of self-direction or not? This is arguably one of the toughest and most important choices you can make as their leader. There are a couple of things at play here: how ready they might be to take on ownership and your own reluctance to let go. Perhaps we can take a lesson from our personal lives.

For those of us who have children, the lines of influence between work and home seem fluid at times. Let's try to make them obvious. When parents first bring the baby home, what is their first lament? "I can't wait until she sleeps through the night." And then what do you hear next? "Boy, I can't wait until he's in kindergarten for the morning." Then it's, "When she's in school all day, maybe I'll be able to get something done around here," and, "I can't wait until I don't have to drive the family taxi to take him to every corner of the city." And, finally, "Won't it be nice when I don't have to pay for everything? She's getting expensive." Our end game is moving from one end of a continuum to another so that our kids end up as happy, healthy, functioning adults who live where? *Somewhere else!* We spend our entire career of parental influence developing their readiness and working our own exit strategy. Who wants to be holding the back of a bike for a 40-year-old?

At work, very rarely do we look to or prepare for the next stage with our team members. How many of us focus on letting go and removing ourselves from the tasks of our team as a necessary, desirable, and laudable achievement? Our research says far too few. It's on *their* minds; it's not on ours. Understand too that autonomy is an incremental process. Just as in sales where we see a certain "rush to a relationship" where the salesperson is desperately seeking to be your pal, in leadership too there can sometimes be a rush to autonomy. In response to thin staffing or maybe just in response to lots of enthusiasm from the follower, leaders, when we do think of it, are often in a hurry to offload work. Any work. Autonomy is not all or nothing. We like to use the analogy of becoming an airplane pilot. At first, the student pilot has very little understanding, let alone skill. The appropriate leadership is the flight instructor saying, "Don't touch anything!" The instructor does all the flying and teaching. As the student learns and observes, perhaps it's now time to let him or her feel the controls. As instruction goes on, the student takes on more and more of the tasks until it becomes time for a solo flight. At that point, the flight instructor won't even be in the airplane. It's a *continuum* of involvement, and our protocol states, that as you lead, consider where you are on the continuum and what your next exit point will be. Where are you now? Are you flying the aircraft while they simply observe, or are they flying the airplane with you on the ground? Make the call.

And, tactically, how do you do it? How do you manage autonomy in the moment? There are two steps:

1. **Jointly acknowledge the task.** Ask your team member to write down the two or three tasks that he or she believes the two of you will be talking about regularly over the next 60 days or so. At the same time, you create the same list from your perspective. What do you believe are the key goals that the two of you will interact on during the following month or two? Now compare the two lists. Are they the same? Let your team member read you his or her list first, and then you read yours. Discuss the two lists and settle on one item to work on right now. At least you're on the same page.

2. **Clarify ownership.** Make it obvious who owns the task or objective. A close friend and colleague, David Specker, of PDC and Associates, is the originator of one of the best catalyst questions ever used in the line of duty, and we recommend it here. Once you've settled on a common understanding of what task brings you together, ask your team member the following question (word for word): *"In reference to this task, where does your authority end and mine begin?"* Now this is the hard part. Be quiet. Don't fill in the silence. The answers you receive will give you a safe, structured opportunity to either reinforce or

realign both of your expectations about who ultimately makes the decisions—for right now.

Your Exit Strategy

Does it seem that sometimes your leadership tactics never quite get beyond *learning*? Does the lift that your efforts initially provide fall flat when you're back to business as usual? Here's why. For over 100 years we've known that it takes many touches to influence, to learn, to change, and to grow—journeys of 1,000 miles take place one step at a time. There's an axiom in the basics of marketing called the law of 29, which says: *We need to receive a message some 29 times before we will adopt or act upon that message.*

Whether it's really 29 or 26 is irrelevant. What matters is that lasting change takes multiple attempts and that a critical mass of early attempts is what is needed to *activate* new behaviors. These attempts are what help move ideas from concept to practice. Your attempts can have the best chance of a positive outcome if they are: *transparent* (no agenda, no ulterior motive), *purposeful* (planned with an impact in mind), and *active* (designed for action, not just consideration). In keeping with the law of 29, we want you to consider your exit strategies. Make empowerment transparent to your team members. Talk about it. The circuitry in all our brains literally fires more intensely when we hear words or say them (and not just think them). The overt discussion of letting go creates a form of psychological contract between those involved in the conversation; that is the intent, the *purpose* of the discussions. And the final ingredient in your exit strategy can be articulated in two words, *data* and *delta*.

Data are individual facts, statistics, or items of information used as a basis for reason, discussion, or calculation. Bring data into your dialogue about letting go. What are the milestones that will take the both of you from flight instruction to solo flight? What *specifically* do you need to see to tell you that your team

155

member is in fact ready for full autonomy? Use the taxonomy of quality, quantity, and time to articulate these milestones.

Delta is quantitative, incremental change. Any time you discuss letting go, look for the delta, look for change, look for a successive approximation, a next step that is close to the milestones you've identified. We can almost always spot growth, if we're looking. The message here about your exit strategy is that it too is incremental and achievable. In our last book, *What Got You Here Won't Get You There—in Sales!*, we advocated change by picking something that matters and attacking it until it doesn't matter anymore. In seeking an exit—from your peoples' responsibilities—pick one thing that matters, and attack it until it doesn't matter anymore.

The word *protocol* comes into play every day in healthcare. You heard from our close associate, Davis Holloway, who is in fact currently battling leukemia, a disease that cripples the immune system. Being unable to combat everyday bacteria or even a simple virus, a strict protocol of neutropenic precautions are followed in treating leukemia patients. Care providers scrub up, glove up, and mask up to maximize the effectiveness of the treatment they undertake and to minimize any chance of infection or harm in the process. A leader's protocol is built on the same foundational reasoning—proven research-based practice designed to maximize effectiveness and minimize the downside. Take the specific steps we've shown you to master being present to address the communication, feedback, and autonomy needs of your people. Follow the leader's protocol.

Unlike many of our other professional interactions as consumers (think airlines, gas stations, banks, or grocery stores), leadership is *not* a self-service business. Leadership is full time, *full service*. Leadership is active. Leadership is personal. Leadership takes energy.

Stay tuned for the rest of the story, to learn how to generate and maintain that energy, in Chapter 10, Happiness Matters: Finding the Energy to Lead.

Happiness Matters: Finding the Energy to Lead

You'll note in the banner of our website, multi-touchperformance.com, and in quite a few other places in our literature, a stylized character just like the one you see on this page. This character is that of *happiness* (actually, with a little bit of *luck* and *fortune* in there as well). A character often represents one's identity, or at least a personal philosophy. Our philosophy of life and work is one of happiness, certainly for ourselves, and more importantly what we can contribute to the happiness of others. In short, we help people with people, to both maximize results, and in the end, to feel good about it.

This philosophy or outlook, like any, reflects the presence of several people in our lives, especially our parents, whose unfailing optimism provides an attitudinal foundation, and mentors like Paul Hersey and Marshall Goldsmith, whose simple truths of acting on purpose and being happy help illuminate happiness as a definable and achievable state—and a viable, learnable life skill. As best we can discern, happiness boils down to prosperity and contentment and is at the very center of all that we do professionally and personally.

Make no mistake. In our thinking, prosperity doesn't mean a lack of hard work, and contentment does not connote freedom from desire or want. Our goal is choosing a path of contentment and prosperity for ourselves and doing everything we can to help others find the same. As you'll see in this final chapter, happiness matters. It matters for a number of reasons, the most important being that happiness enables passion, and passion creates energy. We make the point in the closing of Chapter 9 that leadership is a contact sport. Leadership is personal. Leadership is full time and full service. It takes energy. And this closing chapter is all about how you can find the energy you need to lead. You've learned a great deal so far:

○ The concept of capacity without headcount
○ The loss of our ability to connect with one another
○ The importance of the moment in leading in the next decade
○ What your people want you to know and do
○ Where to target your leadership efforts, and how interaction works
○ How to master being present as the number-one leadership competency
○ A powerfully simple leader's protocol for making every moment count

Now join us for the final journey—finding the energy to lead. How to harness passion, not just create it. How to build a life that includes the ingredients for happiness, passion, and energy.

Happiness, Passion, and Energy

We can learn a lot about happiness by considering its synonyms rather than a simple definition: pleasure, joy, contentedness, satisfaction, cheerfulness, enjoyment, exuberance, optimism, peace of mind, well-being. All are valid; all are accurate. Happiness is personal. For us, it's a state of perceived abundance and contentment. Regardless of definition, what most do seem to agree upon is the connection between happiness and personal energy. Let's take a look at what we know about happiness, its traditional paradigms, and, of course, the science behind it.

Historically, happiness hasn't been all that popular a concept. It wasn't always thought about or spoken of. At one time, it was even considered a sinful pursuit. And even though today happiness enjoys a setting high on a pedestal of desirability, it was only within the second half of the twentieth century that it found its place, especially the idea that our work should somehow be a source of that happiness. Granted, different cultures display and pursue happiness in different ways. Germans differ from Americans; Japanese differ from Australians; Chinese differ from Arabs. Suffice it to say that happiness does matter today, even if we can't quite understand how just yet.

Now make room for modern technology, including brain imaging and mobile apps. Let's find out what scientific method can tell us about happiness. In general, happier people bring more energy to their work in the form of positive attitudes and emotions. This we know. All else being equal, happy people, with more positive energy and passion for their work, tend to perform more effectively.

159

This we also know. We believe that the gray area lies within the approach most people take to finding happiness for themselves. It matters to them personally, it matters to their employer, and the return on happiness can be huge, but perhaps the logic needs reversing.

Current thought seems to suggest that all of us should be able to find happiness and its resultant passion somewhere in our work. Conventional wisdom seems to be that if you aren't satisfied with your labors, and many are not, then you should tap into what you already love and do *that* for a living. According to Cal Newport, an assistant professor at Georgetown University, right now, some 45 percent of our collective workforce is dissatisfied in their jobs. For those under the age of 25, the number is 64 percent. No problem, right? Just do what you love, do what you are passionate about, and all is well (especially in this era that advocates entrepreneurial solutions to anything that ails you). Perhaps not. Stories abound of those who dream of running their own restaurant because they love to cook, those who start a landscaping business because they love to garden. How do you think it works out for them? Usually it doesn't. That is the passion paradox, the belief that the only route to job satisfaction and its many benefits lies within finding the job that will make you happy.

But research tells us that passion is not within the work. The satisfaction isn't within the job. It comes from within *you*. The top situational contingency in job satisfaction is a personal trait known as "core self-evaluation." The most important personal trait for predicting job satisfaction and the passion it brings to the work is simply core self-evaluation. In other words, the primary driver of satisfaction on the job is our satisfaction *with ourselves*. It's not a case of looking to the work to make us happy or give us energy. Success and satisfaction at work lie within harnessing the energy we're capable of generating and maintaining and directing it toward our work. Here are a few more items that caught our attention in researching this topic:

○ Manufactured happiness can be just as powerful as natural happiness. This means that consciously working toward being positive, happy, or satisfied can affect you just as deeply as something positive happening *to* you.
○ Organic happiness, or happiness that takes us by surprise, has roughly a 90-day shelf life. There are very few things that happen to us externally that please us for longer than three months.
○ Frequency trumps intensity. More frequent, less-intense positive experiences have a much stronger, much longer-lasting effect on you and your spirit than a rare but very powerful single event.

So where do we go from here? Happiness brings energy and passion, and we add that to our work, not the other way around. Let's again go to scientific method to find out what happy, passionate people have in common. Among those that consistently score high on core self-evaluation *and* job satisfaction, the common denominators are *ritual, interaction, service,* and *health.*

These are the variables of passion, the building blocks of energy at work or at play. Ritual, interaction, service, health. The inclusion and protection of these in your life will give you the best possible shot at having the energy you need to lead others, the passion you can then bring to making every moment count. We've asked a very special person to give you the benefit of his wealth of education and experience on how to make it happen in your life.

Dan Saferstein, Ph.D., is a licensed psychologist who consults with individuals, families, teams, and organizations. He is an accomplished author in his own right and cites Ann Meyers Drysdale, president and general manager of the Phoenix Mercury and vice president of the Phoenix Suns, and Sue Enquist, former UCLA softball coach, 11-time national champion, 4-time hall of famer among many personal testimonials for his work.

Bring Out the Best: Dan, can you provide your perspective on the use of rituals, social interaction, service or altruism, and health as key strategies for generating and conserving the energy needed to lead or coach?

Dan Saferstein: Let's start with rituals then. They create a predictable rhythm of togetherness for many of us. The idea of a ritual is to make you feel more alive and appreciative. Think about it. Rituals usually celebrate a passage in one way or another, and they give us more than anything the chance to appreciate. Rituals are energizing in that they let us feel gratitude and give thanks, and they provide security, comfort, familiarity. We find that the human psyche is really very conservative and tends to embrace the known. Rituals fill that need. They also often give us a chance to connect with ourselves, if just for a short time. In a leadership sense, the team rituals you might put into place can also help the entire group to form an identity separate from the boss. This is important because people will compete more passionately if they are playing for each other rather than if they are playing only for you. The stronger the leadership *within* your team, the less pressure there will be on you to carry them up the mountain by yourself.

When you speak of service, what comes to mind is that the best coaches and leaders are teachers. They understand that they are there to serve their team rather than their team being there to promote their reputation as the boss. There is no need to worry that your team will lose its competitive edge if you focus more on learning than winning. The competitiveness is already in your people; it doesn't need to come from within you. You've got it

162

right, Don. You accept each of your people as your responsibility and try to bring out the best in them, knowing that the process will bring out the best in you as a leader and a coach.

The word *altruism*, I think, is often misconstrued. Engaging in altruistic acts doesn't mean that you don't get anything out of it. Think about Mother Teresa. It wasn't just the poor of Calcutta who benefitted from her compassionate service. She gained a great deal personally through her service. Altruism infuses meaning into life for many people. Perhaps we look for different things at different stages of our lives. Younger people may be looking to achieve to meet their needs; yet at a later stage we often look for more meaning or significance to what we do. Altruistic acts provide that feedback for us. A higher calling to our labors can be very enriching and energizing. It brings us closer to people and helps us be one with others. Work sometimes doesn't do that for us.

Bring Out the Best: That's very powerful, Dan. There was a book by Bob Buford called *Half Time: Move from Success to Significance* that echoes your sentiment. As we get older and gain a little more business acumen, we tend to look for more meaning in what we do. And it's a big lift whenever we can find it, anywhere in our lives.

Can you provide further observations in terms of how we can generate and even *conserve* energy as coaches and leaders of others?

Dan Saferstein: I have an exercise called "pull back the lens" as a way to conserve focus. I understand that preparation is about details, and execution is about preparation. But it's also important that you know how to pull back the lens as a coach or leader, see the bigger picture, and not be consumed by the details of short-term results. Addictions weaken all relationships including an addiction to work. Addictions make you small-minded and small-hearted. To be an effective leader, you need to have a heart big enough to take in all the people you are trying to lead and also wise enough to not crowd out your loved ones.

One way to increase the size and wisdom of your heart is to expand your emotional repertoire. Instead of just feeling anger, fear, and impatience—the big three of workaholism—see if you can welcome joy or some other emotion that will allow you to better engage your team members. Contrary to popular belief, it can be a huge relief not to take yourself so seriously. The weight of the world is no longer just on your shoulders. Your time and energy don't feel like a scarce commodity that you must constantly guard at all costs.

Another way to conserve energy is to put your time where your values are. Maybe the truth about human connections is that they often involve inconvenience, and if you are determined to have a convenient life, you should probably never let yourself get too close with anyone. Children get it. They just don't understand the relationship that some people have with their work. It makes no sense to them that someone could be so consumed by his job that he (or she) could feel guilty or restless or distracted when he wasn't working. Does that sound familiar? The reality is if you try to get everything done today, you will end up feeling pretty isolated and miserable by tomorrow. So this means you need to *consciously choose whom or what you're going to neglect.* You don't have to be a victim of your career. Treat what is sacred sacredly. Don't keep giving the same apologies about how busy you are because if you recycle an apology enough times, it will eventually become a lie.

Bring Out the Best: Can we combine this approach to conserving energy with the concept of health and the capacity for passion?

Dan Saferstein: Sure, one good way to start taking care of yourself is by getting a good night's sleep. Tonight. Not when the fiscal quarter is over. I find that many leaders get so caught up that they have forgotten how to let go and surrender to the feeling of being exhausted. I realize that coaches and leaders aren't generally in love with the idea of surrendering, but it's much better to surrender to sleep than alcohol or something else that's even worse for you than the exhaustion. If taking care of yourself feels too indulgent, think of it as a sacrifice that you make for your team. Health isn't only about diet and exercise. It's also about maybe finding a way to serve others. There is sufficient evidence to suggest that the givers of the world tend to live longer than the takers, and yet it's hard to truly give to others when you don't take proper care of yourself.

The other guidance for taking care of yourself is to know when to call time-out. Coaches burn out just as players do; leaders the same as followers. If you want your team to feel engaged, you need to feel the same thing inside. You are the psychological compass. That's why your work with yourself is as important as the work you do with your team. Some signs you might be struggling are sleeping too little; drinking too much; getting headaches, stomachaches, or muscle aches; feeling irritable or impatient or alone. Your time-outs can take many different forms. You can go for a run or take a walk. You can have a quiet dinner at home. What you do is less important than the *spirit* and *pace* in which you do it. You can call time-out as a way of keeping problems small. Your leadership career is not a sprint. It is more like a marathon, which means you need to learn how to pace yourself. This is a race you want to last in.

Bring Out the Best: Let's finish on the passion anchor of social interaction. What are your observations?

Don Saferstein: Social interaction can be very good for us, and the top doesn't have to be lonely if you're willing to make room on it for others. Most tops are usually big enough to accommodate

165

plenty of people, providing you don't let your self-importance take up too much room. Keep in mind that you are never alone as a leader or coach unless you *choose* to be alone. It is a myth that the less you need people, the stronger you will be. It is a myth that if you want a job done right, you need to do it yourself. There are other people capable of lightening your load. There are other people capable of appreciating your load if you would open up and tell them about it. One of the greatest lessons that sports teaches us is that a group of people working together can be so much more powerful than a collection of individuals working alone. There is no reason to create a leader's island for yourself. Think of life as a team sport and see where that takes you.

Powerful words, valuable advice. Thank you, Dan. Ritual, interaction, service, and health. Build rituals into your lives—simple behavioral ceremonies, social interaction for its own sake—you don't have to be alone. Be of service to others; you receive back 100-fold, and guard your energy through healthy practice. But what is that exactly? To finish, we have invited one more very, *very* special interview.

Natalie Brown is the director of operations for Todd Durkin Enterprises in San Diego, California. Natalie earned her B.S. degree from the University of Michigan, studied at Oxford University in England, and worked in the applied behavioral sciences as a Master Situational Leadership trainer for years. During that time she consulted with the likes of Chrysler Corporation, McLaren Health, Eddie Bauer, and Aero Postale. She later returned to the university for a master's of science in exercise physiology with certification. She now combines the physical sciences with the behavioral in coaching and training clients under Todd Durkin's mentorship. Athletes such as Drew Brees, Aaron Rogers, and many NFL, MLB, Olympic, and NCAA athletes count themselves among the clients of Todd Durkin's Fitness Quest 10.

Bring Out the Best: Natalie, you've read the powerful words of Dan Saferstein in reference to managing ritual, interaction, service, and health to gain the energy that a leader needs to make every moment count. From a *clinical* perspective, what are the basics of first building and then maintaining our health and our energy to lead, regardless of where we work?

Natalie Brown: There is a lot of noise today about health. Google the word *health* and within 27 one-hundredths of a second you have *4.4 billion* suggestions. Google *exercise* and you get 640 million ideas. *Diet* generates 595 million pages. I'm hoping that some of my ideas will sound familiar to you, but as I said, there is a lot of noise out there. I'm going to give you my top three with what we do right and what we need to stop doing. These apply whether you play for the San Diego Chargers or the LA Clippers, or whether you play pick-up soccer or don't engage in athletics whatsoever.

The top three are *hydration, fuel,* and *movement.*

Again, these apply no matter who you are. Let's take hydration first. I can't say it loud enough, and it's first for a reason: pay attention to drinking enough *water* every day. Not soda, not juices, and not specialty coffees. Water is what we are made of; we need it in our systems and the full functioning of our organs. Did you know that newborns are 75 percent water? Young teens are still 50 to 60 percent water. As we get older, our chemistry changes, but many of the people you meet on any given day are chronically and *clinically* dehydrated. Add any significant level of physical activity to that, and we become seriously dried out. Classic guidelines advocate eight 8-ounce glasses every day. I'm for even more than that if you can stand it, but consider it a minimum.

Fuel is next, and it means anything you put in your mouth that isn't water. And the first thing I'd like to address is *when* you eat, not just what. I'm talking about hunger, and knowing the difference between hunger and craving. Think about it for a moment.

167

We need to recondition ourselves to eat when we are hungry and not just craving. If you aren't sure, ask yourself, "If a veggie I enjoy were right in front of me right now, flavored just the way I like it, would I eat it?" If the answer is no, then you're not hungry. You are craving. Feed hunger, not cravings. It's another conditioned response we've come to accept as normal. It doesn't have to be. Most of our cravings are either for sugar or carbs, and we don't need either one.

Now let's tackle a commonsense approach to food itself. It's only three words—eat real food. If you can't pronounce it, don't eat it. If it wasn't around when your grandparents were your age, don't eat it. When you can, eat foods with fewer than three ingredients. Simplicity is king when it comes to diet, and a counselor at UM I knew used to say, "Eat until you're satisfied, never full." That's very good advice.

The last component of my approach to health is the idea of movement. This is another reflection of your rule of three. Exercise at least three times per week for 60 minutes. That's all. Everyone has heard the advice. Very few follow it. The cool thing about the secret to health is that it's not a secret. I'm not sure where I heard that, but it fits to a T. Engage in an activity until you like it. It takes anywhere from three to eight weeks to ingrain a habit. Most of us scare off long before our body gets a chance to acclimate to the movement. With enough time you can enjoy your activity. If you are at a desk for the majority of the day, make a point to get up and move around. Take a walk to go talk to a coworker instead of sending an e-mail. Go up and down a flight of stairs, or enjoy a brief break out of doors for five minutes. That's all it takes. And ladies, don't just do cardio. Lift weights. It will improve bone density and increase metabolism. And don't worry. Lifting weights will not cause you to bulk up or get big. Just healthy.

Hydration, fuel, and movement. In a nutshell, drink more water, eat more simply and less often, and move more. It's an easy but powerful mantra.

Bring Out the Best: Natalie, that's as useful a treatise on healthy practice as we've ever heard. Thank you. In closing, can I ask you to answer four questions that I've put to many of our other interviewees. Within your context of health and healthy practice, if you could only provide one piece of advice, what would it be? Then, in reference to their health, what should our readers start doing, stop doing, and continue doing?

Natalie Brown: What one thing would I say above all else? Treat your body and your energy as if they were the most important things on the planet, because they are. It is all you have. Treat your body gently by strengthening it daily through an optimal diet, exercise, and allowing yourself the time you need to recharge your batteries.

What should they start doing? Start auditing. Measure, track, and record what you do in reference to your health—your water and calorie intake, your activity levels.

What should they stop doing? Stop expecting to achieve goals in an area that cannot be or that you do not really want to achieve. Set yourself up for success by setting goals that you *know* with small behavioral changes you can achieve.

What one thing should someone continue to do? Continue to want more for yourself in all of these areas. Never settle; never give up. You are reading this book because you care about yourself. Continue *caring*.

The Leader's Daily

For those who aren't musicians or are not *yet* musicians, the word *coda* refers to the concluding passage of a movement or composition. The concluding passage of this work, this coda, is titled The Leader's Daily. In the last chapter we discussed how rituals provide us with energy and comfort. It is our wish that you take away your first leader's ritual right here, right now.

Do you recall the law of 29? It states that it takes a series of touches to promote acceptance and adoption of new behaviors. What follows is a series of short, succinct readings on topics relevant to leading in the moment. Each consists of only a few paragraphs, and the readings are intended as one-a-day readings for a month. Our topics include everything from How to Get Someone to Open Up; Correcting in the Moment; and The Art of Reflection.

There are enough readings on the following 20 pages to get you going, Monday through Friday, for a month. Just five or ten minutes are all it takes to start your day in development.

After that, pick up readings of your own to continue to bring out the best *in you*.

Day 1: How to Get Someone to Open Up

It's obvious that something is bothering one of your team members. It's all over her face (a constant frown). You ask her, "What's wrong?" and the response is, "Nothing. I'm fine." What should you do?

There are two very powerful techniques you can use to help someone open up to you:

The first involves the use of "Tell me about . . . ," and "Describe for me. . . ." Instead of asking what, when, where, and how, leave your question open. Leave *her* a conversational gap to fill. Ask her to, "Tell you about item A," or ask her to "Describe for you" the status of item B.

The second technique involves something far more difficult— seven seconds of silence. Try it sometime; it's not easy. When you ask one of your people to tell you about something, silently count to seven before saying anything. Let her realize that it's safe to answer your question.

Day 2: Correcting in the Moment

If you work in education, healthcare, retail, call centers, or other arenas in which you can't call "time out" to work on a performance issue, then you know just what I mean. You can't put a classroom full of students or a store full of customers on hold. You have no choice, and it's less than ideal, but how can you make the most of it?

The first thing to ask yourself is: Is it *operational* or is it *personal*? If the issue is purely operational, make sure you don't correct someone in front of customers (it's easy to forget that they're even there). If the failing is personal, specifically if your interaction will affect the confidence or motivation of the team member, then find a way to make it *private.*

When you're correcting performance in the moment, it is not enough to let someone know how he's doing right now. You also have to define what you mean by *"now."* Has his performance been low for three days? Three weeks? Three months? And how long is "low" acceptable before it is a problem? It varies by task, but defining the now and then communicating it is *your* responsibility. The payback is that in defining "now" you acknowledge whether you haven't given the problem enough time or whether it's gone on too long.

The first consideration tells you *where* to deal with a performance issue; the second tells you *when.*

Day 3: Leading at the Speed of Life

Are you currently busier than you have ever been? Feeling over-solicited, overscheduled, and overloaded in every arena? At work? At home? Even at play? Are you hard-pressed just to fit it all in? Do you ever catch up? Do you ever get everything on your to-do list done?

It might be economic drivers complicating your life. It could even be cultural or societal pressures behind your daily juggle. Or, as a leader, it might be the complications of the lives of your people simply bleeding over into yours. Does the reason behind it even matter? What counts is a way out:

1. **Give yourself an hour.** When one of your people brings you a problem, ask for a 60-minute buffer for time to respond (or come to their rescue). Let her know that "immediate" solutions come at a high cost and that you need an hour's notice. You will be surprised how many problems solve themselves.
2. **Give yourself 30 minutes.** Schedule it; publish it. Whether it's 7:30 to 8:00 in the morning or the last half hour of the day, put *you* in your Outlook. Do it 12 months in advance. Do it *now*. Claim 6 percent of your day for yourself. You'll be surprised at how much 30 minutes can do.
3. **Give yourself a rest.** Create a "to-stop" list. What can you simply stop doing, delegate, or reconfigure to lighten your load? It's there. Find it and get rid of it.

Day 4: Delivering Structure as a Leader

Part of your role as a leader of others entails the delivery of structure or direction. Because you are responsible for the output of others, you are often necessarily accountable for an alignment of expectations—aligning their expectations to yours.

The most effective method of doing this is through a logical pattern of communication—a *template* that can be followed consistently, either in spoken words or in writing. Three elements offer the best communication pattern for delivering structure:

○ **5 plus or minus 2.** One or two ideas are rarely enough, and eight to ten are far too many. At whatever level of complexity or detail you find yourself, three to seven messages are ideal—enough for understanding, but not too much for execution.

○ **Who, what, when, and how.** In most cases, providing structure includes some variation of who's involved, what results are desired, and probably most importantly *how* they might be achieved.

○ **Bullets or numbers.** When you record the message in any written form, consider whether to use bullets or numbers. If you require a specific sequence or priority, use numbers. Otherwise, bullets are all you need.

Day 5: Delivering Support as a Leader

Effective leadership means that the work gets done and that followers feel good about it. Part of ensuring commitment as well as performance from your people involves the concept of *empathy* and your ability to deliver support. Perhaps better stated, to ensure that your people *feel* supported.

Empathy is being aware of or sensitive to the feelings, thoughts, and experiences of another. The empathy connection between you and a follower remains intact when he believes that you understand his perspective and experience and that you care. Period.

To deliver effective supportive behavior to your people:

○ What can you do or say to communicate that you *understand* their experience, their point of view (notice we didn't say "agree with" them; just that you understand)?

○ What will you say or do to communicate that you care about their experience, their perspective?

Delivering support isn't just speaking in a friendly tone of voice. It is working little by little to maintain a very real, very natural human connection.

Day 6: If It Feels Good, You Probably Shouldn't Say It

"If it feels good, you probably shouldn't say it," recently appeared in a listing of favorite quotes and has been haunting me ever since I saw it. While the original source is lost to me, I can translate what it meant to me as a leader, and perhaps to you as well.

You probably shouldn't say it if:

○ It's going to feel good only to you; develop capacity in others, not your ego
○ It's nothing more than name-calling (idiot, jerk, you fill in the blank)
○ It's labeling (lazy or disorganized) instead of specifying behaviors
○ You are saying it to anyone other than the individual in question

While we're sure we could all come up with a lot more examples, what is painfully obvious is the terrible waste this is of a leader's time and energy in a job that requires so much of both.

Day 7: Creating an Environment for Influence

Consider this situation: You're trying to make a point with one of your people, and a third party walks up with a "quick question." Or you see an important realization dawning in a team member's eyes, when your iPhone rings, your laptop chimes, or conversations intrude from the next cubicle. How much do we really lose to distractions? Is it merely inconvenience or a given in twenty-first century living?

Perhaps today's technology contains an analogy for us. Your computer contains a RAM (random access memory) chip used for temporarily storing information as it carries out operations. Our brains have one too. Our "working memory" is what we use to interact with others, and we only have a set amount of it. The sounds and movements of our surroundings can indeed take up our interpersonal RAM and leave us too distracted to engage effectively.

To maximize the effectiveness of your influence environment, be aware of:

○ **Physical comfort.** See to the physical comfort of those you're speaking with. Comfortable seats and even refreshments are important.
○ **Distractions.** Consciously eliminate noise, unnecessary movement, and interruptions. We can try to cope with or ignore distractions, but we can't not see or hear them.

Minimize distractions and you'll find your interactions more effective, more engaging, and more powerful.

Day 8: Promote to Potential; Lead to Performance

Is one of your staff members not living up to his or her potential (or perhaps, are more than one not doing so)? You have high expectations, and your employees seem to have all the requisite qualities, but it's just not happening? Maybe you've found similar disappointment in your *personal* life—the ideal partner or offspring that just doesn't live up to your image of him or her.

The root cause in either case is usually one of living, and especially leading, to potential, to what we want things to be and not to what they are. We *will* act based upon our assumptions about others. The solution then lies in basing our assumptions (and therefore our actions) on data, not just desire:

○ **The bigger the stretch, the greater the risk.** If the move is a big one, expect to be significantly involved. Promoting someone to where she has no direct experience will make your life more complex, not less.

○ **Provide the involvement her performance merits now.** The payoff, like the realization of her potential, lies somewhere in the future. Communicate what you want, and stay with her.

○ **Seek help, not just "an accomplice."** When we're inconvenienced or frustrated, we too often look for someone to validate our current tactics, even though they are failing us. When you ask for an outside opinion, listen, don't debate.

Sometimes we do the wrong thing for all the right reasons. The route to success often comes with keeping all thoughts of tomorrow in check and leading to what is, not what could be.

Day 9: A Leader's Guide to Losing Weight

What do you tend to put off at work? What and *whom* do you tend to avoid: People with whom you feel tension? Higher-stakes decision making? Starting or ending a significant chapter in your professional life? Is it owning a mistake you've made or acknowledging feelings or insecurities?

Carrying too much "weight" can kill you. Carrying too much "wait" exacts its toll in productivity, piece of mind, and personal effectiveness. At some point "wait and see" is simply avoidance, not strategy. What can you do about it?

○ **Write it down.** Articulate in writing what and whom you currently avoid, be it people, decisions, or feelings.
○ **Take a first step with someone.** Approach people involved and acknowledge your avoidance.
○ **Take a last step with someone.** Don't be afraid to let go of the "wait" in your life.

Completion will set you free. You'll be surprised how good you feel, and how much more effective you can be for those who count on you.

Day 10: Getting Comfortable with Tension

The role of leader involves achievement through others, often many others. And given enough leadership experience, you will find yourself working with people who are not happy with you. You will find yourself coping with interpersonal tension and depending on your organizational climate. It may feel that you are always coping with tension—that no one is ever happy. You can't eliminate it, but you *can* get comfortable with it:

○ **Delay is a strategy; use it.** Anger takes five to seven minutes to resolve physiologically (emotionally it can take years). Schedule resolution instead of reacting in the moment.

○ **Hope is not a strategy.** Stop wishing for a better past.

○ **Detach your "self"; it ain't personal.** Stop dwelling on the impact on you. Make it all about "them," and the tension magically evaporates.

○ ***Melt* the ice; don't try to break it.** You'll be surprised at what a little kindness can do right now (start with exercising more control than usual over your *non*verbal messages).

○ **Take the home-field advantage; meet where *you* are most comfortable.** Whether it's your office or the cafeteria, make sure your surroundings don't add to the problem.

Day 11: In Search of Motivation, Part 1

Over the long term, all of us know that motivation needs to come from within. We also know that as leaders sometimes our people aren't motivated from within. Leader as motivator is a role we'd better get comfortable with. It can be frustrating, it can be maddening, and it often feels like a shot in the dark.

Perhaps you can become more comfortable if you better understand your options. We have found extrinsic motivation best expressed in terms of what you give versus what employees want:

o **Coercion: Give/Don't Want.** In this first option you are giving someone what he doesn't want (such as punishment). Accept that in rare circumstances, one of your options involves the application of a negative consequence.

o **Withholding: Don't Give/Want.** The motivator here lies in not providing what employees desire until you receive the behaviors you are looking for.

o **Rescue: Don't Give/Don't Want.** The rescue motivator essentially lies in taking away the pain that another person feels. Relieving discomfort can be a strong driver of another's performance.

o **Reinforcement: Give/Want.** This fourth and most effective option directly targets the behaviors you want from another, as opposed to eliminating those you don't want.

Our next release—Motivation, Part 2—deals with selecting consequences, both positive and negative.

Day 12: In Search of Motivation, Part 2

In this second look at motivation, we'd like to focus on the idea of consequences—pleasure *and* pain—that you put in place as the leader to move another person toward what you want. Understand first that external consequences create movement, not *motivation*. Let's face it. Who is the one who's motivated in the equation? You are. You want the outcome, and through these consequences you can create significant and valuable movement toward it. Positive and negative consequences can be very effective if you craft them to be:

○ **Personal.** Don't emphasize the impact of someone's behavior on others. Concentrate on the direct connection to the one doing the behaving. What will be different in her life?

○ **Immediate.** Say what will happen as a result now, not later. Articulating the long term may excite you, but others will gravitate toward what they believe will happen in the short term.

○ **Certain.** If employees don't really believe you, what you say won't move them. Be prepared with the reward as promised or the sanction as threatened.

In our next release—Motivation, Part 3—we finish with how to move others from *within*.

Day 13: In Search of Motivation, Part 3

In closing out our coverage of motivation, let's go back to the first sentence from Day 11: "Over the long term, all of us know that motivation needs to come from within." We've given you rules and tools to consider in motivating others, tips for balancing extrinsic consequences, and how you might create movement in another toward outcomes *you* desire as the leader. Now the question is, What moves people from within? What do we know about the intrinsic needs that drive all of us?

Research has shown that there is usually one of three basic needs that any of your team members might be hardwired to want to satisfy: a need for performance, a need for people, or a need for power:

o **Performance.** Do employees respond best when given the opportunity for significant achievement?
o **People.** Is it the affiliation with others in the group that excites them day in and day out?
o **Power.** Are they driven toward freedom of decision making and execution above all else?

Find out what drives your team members *from within*. Don't be afraid to ask them. Discover and leverage what naturally pulls them to perform, and you won't have to push.

Day 14: Just Because You Are Uncomfortable

We often hear participants and coaching clients admit that certain leader behaviors, while desirable, make them uncomfortable. They claim, "I know I need to be more assertive, but it's just not me," or, "I know that listening better would help me, but it's not my style." Our response? Get comfortable with being uncomfortable.

Positive behavioral change requires discomfort. When you diet, you feel hungry, but it's still you. When you exercise, especially later in life, you definitely experience discomfort, but it's still you. Professional development and new behaviors might cause anxiety, *but it's still you*:

- **Make a choice.** Physiologically, fear and excitement are identical. Choose what you want to feel.
- **Advertise.** Getting the word out takes the pressure off. Secrecy only raises tension.
- **Forgive.** When old habits creep back in, forgive and forget. You would for another, so why not for you?

Day 15: Delegating or Dumping—Eye of the Beholder

To me, the incident felt like delegation: turning over responsibility and authority for decision making and implementation. To the employee, the incident seemed like dumping: my freeing myself from unimportant, boring, or simply distracting administrative trivia. Which was it? In the world of leadership, beauty or beast lies in the eye of the beholder. It wasn't delegating; it was dumping.

Now what? I can't take back what happened. I don't get second takes on first impressions. How might I manage such situations more effectively in the future? Go ahead and do it. Just do it right:

○ **Who benefits and how?** Have an honest discussion about your needing to free up your time, while considering how the transfer of work builds business maturity for the other person. Tell it as you see it.

○ **Make it a *twofer*.** Delegate what you need to be free of along with a task that the other person is keen to take on. It will cost you energy at first, but she will take ownership of both very quickly.

○ **Check your casual comments.** Make sure you don't sabotage yourself with offhand remarks about how disagreeable the task is. If you drop remarks about what a pain it is, how will she come to view it?

○ **Use the power of "thank you."** A regular expression of appreciation takes the rough edge off almost any task. When they know you value her effort, the task can take on more value.

Day 16: Encouragement—Incentive or Reward?

You treat everyone fairly. Always. The same performance management system applies to everyone, yet some people respond positively, while others go backwards. Let's try to figure out why and what to do about it. Perhaps a dictionary contains the answer:

In~cen~tive = something to incite another to action or greater effort

Re~ward = something in return for a deed or service rendered

When do *you* encourage someone? Is yours a constant effort to move him toward higher performance? Or do you target your support to coincide with a desired outcome that has already been achieved? Think about it for a moment. Are you more often there for him before or after the fact? We find many leaders use up so much of their energy "pushing" for performance that they have very little left for acknowledging, recognizing, and thanking once they get it:

- **You are the most powerful reward you have.** Studies prove that your encouragement and recognition carry far more weight than any annual performance matrix ever designed.
- **Save some for later.** Don't use up all your interpersonal energy trying to convince or persuade someone to perform. Genuine praise, especially unannounced upon completion of a job, can last forever.

Day 17: Fighting for Attitude

Do you find yourself mentally dragging these days? Do you experience anger over incompetence, along with an equal measure of frustration over organizational handcuffs? You're not alone. Negative thoughts regularly pass through our minds, and many of the messages we're exposed to every day are negative. We live in a divided world.

People often ask me, "Which is more important to a leader? Attitude or behavior?" My response? Your attitude comes first. It affects *you*, and your resultant behavior then spreads it around. My message? Fight for your attitude. Don't let others hijack your internal dialogue.

At~ti~tude = a tendency or orientation of the mind

○ **First, turn it off.** Turn away from news with an agenda on TV or the Internet. Walk past the pity-party table in the office cafeteria. Minimize the negative messages you expose yourself to.
○ **Second, turn it around.** The act of verbalizing a negative thought reinforces it, so don't say it. Instead, take out a Post-It note and write down the negative thought. Then cross it out and write the positive thought that completely counters it. This is the thought to say out loud as you get back to work.

Day 18: The Power of Suggestion

Picture this: One of your team members tells you of a problem. She provides the big picture and all the details and then comes a lull. You have the solution to her dilemma. What do you say next? I don't mean in general terms. I mean specifically—exactly—what do you say next?

For many of us the response begins with, "What you should do is . . ." or, "You know what you should do?" or, "Why don't you . . ." or, "If I were you, I would . . ."

Instead, access the power of *the word* "suggestion." Reply with, "Would you like a suggestion?" And then wait for a response! You will be pleasantly surprised at its effectiveness:

○ **The power comes from respect.** Jumping in at the first chance communicates that the employee is incapable of solving it for himself. Are you really the only one who could possibly possess the answer?

○ **The power comes from permission.** The act of asking for and receiving permission from another increases his acceptance of your ideas and sharpens his listening skills, too.

Day 19: Defuse, Not Defeat

You become involved in an argument with a team member, a colleague, or even a loved one. What do you do in this ultracompetitive culture? What is your natural response? Win. Win the argument. If it is really important, you want to win it. If it is of no consequence at all, you still want to win it.

People get hurt in arguments. If *you* win, they get hurt. If *they* win, you get hurt. Even petty arguments carry anger and damage.

How about win less and learn more. In most cases we focus on the battle and not on the combatants or casualties. Try that shift in perspective; try a new response to anger:

- **Keep it level.** Keeping your voice and eyes level counters the urge to escalate the argument. Don't raise your voice's volume or pitch, and don't raise your eyebrows.
- **Restate their point of view.** Ask the person you're arguing with whether you've got it right. The first objective is understanding, not agreement.
- **Ask.** Specifically, ask her, "What would you like me to do?" Then wait for a response. You won't solve it all, but the problem takes the hit, not the players.

Day 20: So What? Now What? The Art of Reflection

There were 200,000 texts sent every *second* in 2011. There were also some 107 *trillion* e-mails that went across our collective desk in that same 12-month period. How many of them showed up in your inbox? How often were you tagged every day?

We know we're losing the capacity to connect with others and with so much information hitting us every day, we're losing the ability to even connect with ourselves. We're losing the capacity to reflect—to *learn* from information we receive. Perhaps two very simple questions can force a moment of reflection:

1. **So what?** When you see, hear, or receive information, ask yourself, "So what? What makes it meaningful? Why does it matter to me?" These questions allow you to analyze and evaluate.
2. **Now what?** The second query, "Now what? What should I do with this information?" is about integrating the data into what you do, and the answer is multiple choice: Discard—the information has no value; Divert—the information is of value to someone else; Respond—the data are valuable to me and require further involvement.

The Mindful Attention and Awareness Scale (MAAS)

Day-to-Day Experiences

Instructions: Below is a collection of statements about your everyday experiences. Using the 1–6 scale, please indicate how frequently or infrequently you currently have each experience. Please answer according to what *really reflects* your experience rather than what you think your experience should be. Please treat each item separately from every other item.

1	2	3	4	5	6
Almost always	Very frequently	Somewhat frequently	Somewhat infrequently	Very infrequently	Almost never

I could be experiencing some emotion and not be conscious of it until some time later.	1	2	3	4	5	6
I break or spill things because of carelessness, not paying attention, or thinking of something else.	1	2	3	4	5	6
I find it difficult to stay focused on what's happening in the present.	1	2	3	4	5	6
I tend to walk quickly to get where I'm going without paying attention to what I experience along the way.	1	2	3	4	5	6
I tend not to notice feelings of physical tension or discomfort until they really grab my attention.	1	2	3	4	5	6
I forget a person's name almost as soon as I've been told it for the first time.	1	2	3	4	5	6
It seems that I am "running on automatic," without much awareness of what I'm doing.	1	2	3	4	5	6
I rush through activities without being really attentive to them.	1	2	3	4	5	6
I get so focused on the goal I want to achieve that I lose touch with what I'm doing right now to get there.	1	2	3	4	5	6
I do jobs or tasks automatically, without being aware of what I'm doing.	1	2	3	4	5	6
I find myself listening to someone with one ear, doing something else at the same time.	1	2	3	4	5	6
I drive places on "automatic pilot" and then wonder why I went there.	1	2	3	4	5	6
I find myself preoccupied with the future or the past.	1	2	3	4	5	6
I find myself doing things without paying attention.	1	2	3	4	5	6
I snack without being aware that I'm eating.	1	2	3	4	5	6

MAAS Scoring: To score the scale, simply compute a mean (average) of the 15 items. Higher scores reflect higher levels of dispositional mindfulness.

INDEX

ABOUT THE AUTHORS

Don Brown

Whether writing, presenting, coaching, or selling, Don Brown has dedicated his career to influence effectiveness—period. Bilingual and experienced at the executive and line-level alike, you see the results of his work across dozens of industries, including brewing, automotive, airline, banking, and pharmaceuticals.

With over 30 years working in the industry, Mr. Brown is heavily experienced in all phases of major performance systems, from research and design to facilitation and coaching. Working with customers such as Anheuser-Busch, Dell Computers, Ford Motor Company, US Airways and United Airlines, Harley-Davidson Motor Company, Jaguar Cars, Compuware Corporation, SYKES, and Hilton Hotels, Don is accustomed to working domestically and internationally across all functional disciplines. He takes great pride in his longstanding customer relationships, some still running strong after more than 20 years.

Mr. Brown is now releasing the new *Multi-Touch Performance*™ products and services. Based on his in-depth customer research and the premise that it takes several touches to learn, to serve, to sell, and to lead, Don integrates the best of the best into a powerful sequence for human skills development.

Don cherishes his work and mentorship under Paul Hersey and Marshall Goldsmith as the solid foundation of his success. Affiliated with Dr. Hersey for over 25 years, Don coauthored *Situational Service*®—*Customer Care of the Practitioner* with Paul, and has worked hand-in-hand with him to create several highly successful training programs, including *Situational Service*®, *From Vision to Results*™, *Situational Leadership*® *in a Team Environment*, *Situational Selling*®—*Creating Readiness to Buy*, and *Performance Readiness*®.

Mr. Brown has recently coauthored *What Got You Here Won't Get You There—in Sales!* with Marshall Goldsmith (McGraw-Hill, September 2011) and is currently releasing *Bring Out the Best in Every Employee—How to Engage Your Whole Team by Making Every Leadership Moment Count* (McGraw-Hill, 2012).

Don earned an honors degree in foreign languages from Michigan State University and a Masters in Management with Dr. Hersey at California American University. Having lived and studied at the University of Seville in Spain, Don works regularly in English and Spanish in Europe and Latin America. He lives in Ann Arbor, Michigan. Contact Don at dbrown@multitouchperformance.com.

Bill Hawkins

Bill Hawkins is an expert in leadership development and executive coaching. He is a founding member of the Marshall Goldsmith Group and has worked with over 20 Fortune 500 companies in 17 countries. Bill has designed and facilitated leadership education workshops for corporate clients on five continents. He also coaches leaders individually to increase personal effectiveness. Bill began his career with a division of Johnson & Johnson. He then joined Boston Scientific as director and then vice president of sales and marketing. With his blend of consulting and corporate management experience, Bill brings a breadth of understanding and insight to real-world situations.

Bill's clients include Acushnet, American Express, Ashland, AT&T, Bloomberg, Boeing, Boston Scientific, Budget Rent a Car, CalPERS, Cisco, ChevronTexaco, Cox Enterprises, C R Bard, Credit Suisse First Boston Bank, DirecTV, Dreyer's Grand Ice Cream, Exelon, Federal Reserve Bank, Ford Motor Company, FTI Consulting, GlaxoSmithKline, Hitachi (America), Internal Revenue Service, Johnson & Johnson, Labatt Breweries, Kodak, Kerzner International, KPMG, Las Vegas Metro Police Department, Marathon Oil Company, Martha Stewart Living, Mead Johnson, MGM–Mirage Hotels, Motorola, New York Stock Exchange, Nortel, Northrop Grumman, Oracle, Pfizer, PNC Bank, Raytheon, Sanofi-Aventis, Sterling Jewelers, TaylorMade-Adidas, Texas Instruments, Toyota, Union Pacific Railroad, Washington Mutual Financial Services, and Weyerhaeuser.

Aside from his work with major corporations, Bill has donated his services to the International Red Cross/Red Crescent, the New York Association for New Americans, and the Girl Scouts of the U.S.A.

Bill holds a BS from Drake University and an MBA from Indiana University. He is member of the Peter Drucker Foundation "Thought Leader's Forum," a Distinguished Fellow at the "Global Leadership Development Center" at Alliant University, and is listed in Who's Who in International Business. He is a contributing author in the Peter Drucker Foundation book *The Organization of the Future* (Jossey-Bass, 1997). He is also a contributing author in *Coaching for Leadership* (Jossey-Bass, 2003), *Change Champion's Fieldguide* (Best Practice Publications, 2008), and *What Got You Here Won't Get You There—in Sales!* (McGraw-Hill, 2012).